C000282508

PUB STROLLS IN
BERKSHIRE

Nick Channer

COUNTRYSIDE BOOKS
NEWBURY BERKSHIRE

COUNTRYSIDE BOOKS
3 Catherine Road
Newbury, Berkshire

To view our complete range of books,
please visit us at
www.countrysidebooks.co.uk

ISBN 1 85306 779 2

Designed by Graham Whiteman
Maps and photographs by the author

Typeset by Techniset Typesetters, Newton-le-Willows
Produced through MRM Associates Ltd., Reading
Printed by Woolnough Bookbinding Ltd., Irthlingborough

Contents

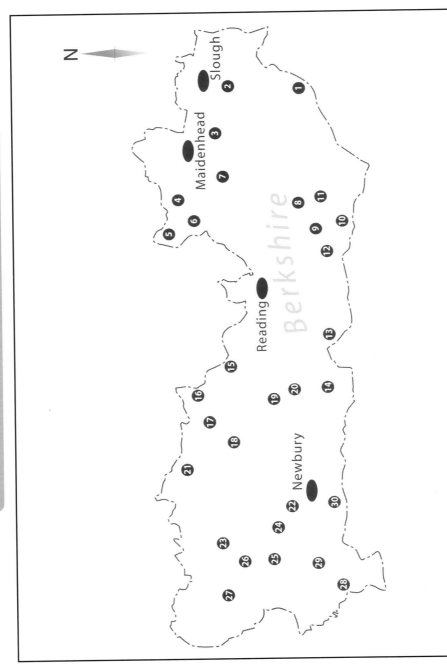

AREA MAP SHOWING LOCATION OF THE WALKS

PUBLISHER'S NOTE

We hope that you obtain considerable enjoyment from this book; great care has been taken in its preparation. However, changes of landlord and actual closures are sadly not uncommon. Likewise, although at the time of publication all routes followed public rights of way or permitted paths, diversion orders can be made and permissions withdrawn.

We cannot, of course, be held responsible for such diversion orders and any inaccuracies in the text which result from these or any other changes to the routes nor any damage which might result from walkers trespassing on private property. We are anxious though that all details covering the walks are kept up to date and would therefore welcome information from readers which would be relevant to future editions.

The simple sketch maps that accompany the walks in this book are based on notes made by the author whilst checking out the routes on the ground. However, for the benefit of a proper map, we do recommend that you purchase the relevant Ordnance Survey sheet covering your walk. The Ordnance Survey maps are widely available, especially through booksellers and local newsagents.

To me, Berkshire is a classic English shire. It may be small and densely populated but within its boundaries lies a variety of fine scenery – from the remains of the ancient Windsor Forest in the east to the great sweeps of windswept downland in the west. In between there are gentle river valleys and some of the prettiest countryside in the south of England. If you joined the county's many footpaths and tracks together, it would represent a memorable journey, providing a fascinating insight into a changing way of life. During the last 250 years or so, in keeping with the rest of Britain, the map of Berkshire has gradually changed as canals, roads and railway lines began to thread their way across the county. As the age of transport dawned, what we now know as the A4 was then established as the Bath Road. Running parallel to it through Berkshire came two other lines of communication: Brunel's Great Western Railway marches cross-country towards Bristol, and the Kennet and Avon Canal cuts through the heart of West Berkshire. Today, a sprawling mass of motorways, busy roads and out-of-town shopping centres separates the county from its distant past.

Against this tide of change, however, the simple pleasure of walking remains the only way to understand and appreciate the countryside and we are fortunate in Berkshire to be blessed with a surviving network of ancient paths and tracks which evolved over the years as a vital means of communication. Different generations used these routes as they went to work in the fields and factories, or travelled to school, market or church, and to surrounding towns and villages. With a little effort, I have come up with 30 strolls that, in every sense, reflect the best of Berkshire. They are all easy and undemanding routes, requiring little or no experience, and they are all perfect for a summer's evening, a Sunday afternoon in autumn or a frosty morning in winter. Every route starts and finishes at a pub where you will find a good choice of food and drink.

Permission has been given for cars to be left whilst you do the walks, but I would urge you to check with the landlord before setting out. If you decide to opt for roadside parking, please be careful not to block any exits or entrances. In addition, brief details about places of interest within easy driving distance of the walk are given to help you plan a full day out if you wish. The book includes detailed route-finding directions but always take a good map – preferably the Ordnance Survey Explorer series.

All that remains now is for me to wish you happy walking in this beautiful county – and enjoy the pubs!

Nick Channer

Sunningdale
The Nags Head

| MAP: OS EXPLORER 160 (GR 953676) | **WALK 1** | DISTANCE: 4 MILES |

DIRECTIONS TO START: THE NAGS HEAD STANDS IN THE CENTRE OF SUNNINGDALE VILLAGE, NOT TO BE CONFUSED WITH MORE MODERN SUNNINGDALE ON THE A30. FOLLOW THIS ROAD BETWEEN BAGSHOT AND ENGLEFIELD GREEN AND FOLLOW THE SIGNS FOR THE VILLAGE, WHICH LIES TO THE NORTH OF THE A30. **PARKING:** OUTSIDE THE PUB AND ALONG THE STREET.

Think of east Berkshire and you think of Ascot, Sunningdale and Virginia Water. This corner of the county was developed in the early years of the 20th century. Cutting through the leafy suburbs, the A30 made it a fashionable place in which to live and, today, it remains a popular address, even if property prices are among the highest in the country. Despite the high density of housing, the area boasts a network of woodland paths and peaceful tracks radiating away from urban development and busy roads. Our route begins in Sunningdale village and then cuts through the Wentworth Estate, famous for its sprawling golf course. On the return leg, the walk passes close to Fort Belvedere where Edward VIII signed the abdication document in December 1936. Further on is Coworth Park, which is partly owned by the Brunei Government and run as a polo centre. The house is built in the style of a medieval Swiss farmhouse.

The Nags Head

Harvey's, the Sussex-based brewery, is not that familiar to Berkshire drinkers. Perhaps even more surprising is that the Nags Head at Sunningdale is the only Harvey's pub in this part of the world. Its precise age is unknown but it was the village dairy in the days when milk was delivered by horse and cart. Its stable block is now a storage area for the pub. This is a traditional drinker's hostelry, with food available only at lunchtime and not at all on Sunday. The menu is varied and wholesome and you can expect the likes of scampi, egg and chips, filled jacket potatoes, baguettes, chicken curry, lasagne, Cumberland sausage, cod fillet and chilli con carne. Children and dogs are welcome and large parties are asked to book. The Nags Head is open all day. Telephone: 01344 622725.

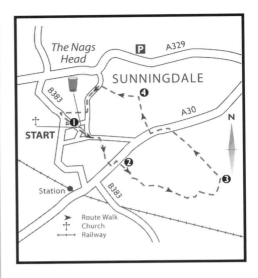

The Walk

① From the Nags Head turn left and follow the High Street, keeping the Anglican church on your right and the Baptist church on the left. Pass Church Road and continue along Bedford Lane. Cross a brook and turn right by some bungalows. Take the path to the A30 and turn left. Walk along to a sign on the right for Shrubs Hill Lane and Onslow Road.

② Follow the path to a junction by a fence and turn right by the bridleway/footpath sign. Curve left, making for a roundabout. Swing left on reaching it and look for a footpath next to a house called Highgate. Follow it through the woodland and when you join a wider path on a bend, keep left. Skirt the golf course, cutting between trees and bracken, and when you emerge from the woodland, follow the path across the fairways, keeping left at a junction by a bunker. Veer left at the first fork, into the trees, and follow the path to a junction with a tarmac drive.

③ Turn left and pass through the exclusive Wentworth Estate. On reaching the A30, turn left and follow the road west. Walk down to the Berkshire/Surrey border and turn sharp right at a right of way. Follow the shaded

PLACES OF INTEREST NEARBY

Virginia Water is a popular attraction on the Berkshire/Surrey border. The lake, which you can circumnavigate on foot, covers about 160 acres and was developed in the middle of the 18th century for the Duke of Cumberland after his victory at Culloden.

Coworth Park

path and beyond the trees you reach the buildings of Coworth Park.

④ Draw level with a bridge, turn left and follow the path across the parkland, crossing a track on the far side. Enter the trees, turn left at the road and pass some houses. Turn right to join a byway by Sunningdale Bowling Club. Keep to a tarmac drive and continue ahead. Turn left at the road, then veer left after a few paces at the fork. Return to the inn.

Windsor
The Donkey House

MAP: OS EXPLORER 160 (GR 967773)	WALK 2	DISTANCE: 2½ MILES

DIRECTIONS TO START: WINDSOR LIES JUST OFF THE M4 (JUNCTION 6). FOLLOW THE SIGNS FOR THE TOWN CENTRE AND MAKE FOR WINDSOR AND ETON RIVERSIDE STATION. HEAD FOR THE RIVERBANK BEHIND IT AND THE PUB IS A SHORT DISTANCE ALONG ON THE RIGHT.
PARKING: THERE IS NO CAR PARK AT THE PUB. HOWEVER, THERE IS A PUBLIC CAR PARK NEXT TO THE STATION, AND VARIOUS OTHER CAR PARKS IN THE TOWN.

You could spend a whole day in Windsor and still not see everything. It is one of those fascinating English towns that is capable of revealing something new and surprising wherever you look. Windsor Castle, founded as a fortress by William the Conqueror, is the town's most famous landmark. The castle has been substantially altered and extended over the centuries, but the most recent work undertaken followed the much publicised fire of 1992. Many of our most famous royal figures are closely associated with Windsor – both in life and death. Queen Elizabeth the Queen Mother's funeral cortege made its way through the streets of the town in the spring of 2002, *en route* to St George's Chapel. Another historic feature of Windsor is the Guildhall, designed at the end of the 17th century by Sir Thomas Fitch and completed by Sir Christopher Wren, who lived in the town. This fascinating heritage trail, starting and finishing by the Thames, explores Windsor's historic corners and hidden backwaters.

The Donkey House

This popular riverside pub is open all day at the weekend, though no food is available on Saturday and Sunday evenings. Burgers, sandwiches and jacket potatoes feature among the snacks, while the main menu offers the likes of scampi, 8 oz rump steak and vegetable curry. Large parties should book. Preferably no children, and dogs are not permitted when food is being served. Telephone: 01753 620010.

The Walk

① On leaving the pub, make for the Thames ahead, turn right and follow Romney Walk, restored in 1992-93. Cross the railway bridge, looking to the right for a good view of Windsor and Eton Riverside station with the castle dominating the scene. Cross the station car park, keeping along the edge of Home Park. Turn right at Datchet Road and make for the station.

② From the front of the station, walk along to the pedestrian crossing and just by the junction is the King George V memorial, unveiled in 1937. Leave Datchet Road here and follow Thames Street as it runs below the castle. The road swings right, passing the Theatre Royal before curving left by the Olde King and Castle pub. On the left here is the Curfew Tower, which contains the bells for St George's Chapel.

③ On the left, further up on Castle Hill, is the famous statue of Queen Victoria. Turn left here towards the castle, then right into Church Street. Turn right at the next junction towards the Guildhall, then turn right into Market Street. Pass the Crooked Tearooms and swing left into Queen Charlotte Street. At 51 feet and 10 inches, this is recorded as the shortest street in Britain.

④ Turn left into the High Street and pass the Guildhall. Continue beyond Windsor

PLACES OF INTEREST NEARBY

Frogmore House, set in the private Home Park, is one of a number of attractions within the Windsor area, being renowned for its splendid landscaped garden and 18th-century lake. Queen Victoria wrote of it: 'All is peace and quiet and you only hear the hum of bees, the singing of the birds.' Frogmore is open on a limited number of days during the year. Call the Tourist Information Centre for more details on places to visit. Telephone: 01753 743900 or email: Windsor.tic@rbwm.gov.uk parish church and follow the road to the junction. Curve right into Sheet Street, then turn right into Victoria Street and walk along to Bachelors Acre. Turn right at the fountains, go up the steps and take the path to the left of a house bearing a plaque. Make for the road and cross over into Mellor Walk, following it left to reach the library. Continue into Sun Passage and then right to reach Chariots Place. Follow the paved walkway to the road and turn right.

⑤ Cross at the lights, turn left into St Leonards Road, then right into Trinity Place. Facing you now is the Garrison church. Keep to the right of it and make for Princess Christian's Hospital, named after Queen Victoria's daughter and now a private hospital. Cross Clarence Road, into Clarence Crescent, passing lines of striking villas. This

Windsor Guildhall

corner of Windsor is reminiscent of a typical London square. Turn right at the next junction and follow Alma Road to the junction with Arthur Road. Cross over and continue along Alma Road, passing under the railway bridge. Cross the coach park into Alexandra Gardens and make for a plane tree enclosed by a shelter. Beyond it is the road. Cross it to the riverside path and turn right. Make for the Town Bridge, passing Sir Christopher Wren's house, now a hotel, on the right. Continue ahead at the bridge and return to the Donkey House.

Holyport
The George

MAP: OS EXPLORER 160
(GR 891777)

WALK 3

DISTANCE: 3 MILES

DIRECTIONS TO START: FROM MAIDENHEAD AND THE M4, HEAD SOUTH ON THE A330. WHEN YOU REACH THE VILLAGE GREEN AT HOLYPORT, LOOK FOR THE GEORGE ON THE LEFT.
PARKING: THE PUB HAS ITS OWN CAR PARK. THERE IS ALSO ROOM TO PARK IN THE VILLAGE.

Between Maidenhead and Windsor lie tracts of pretty countryside and woodland. This easy stroll explores these quiet acres of the county, heading out of Holyport towards Moneyrow Green and Fifield and then returning to the village across fields and along farm tracks. The last leg of the walk allows you to see Holyport at close hand. This classic English village, once the home of Nell Gywnn, is one of Berkshire's prettiest. Have a look at the Belgian Arms in Holyport Street. Before the First World War the inn was known as the Eagle – the sign depicting a Prussian eagle. At the time of the war, there was a POW camp nearby and, out on their exercises, the Germans would pause to salute the eagle as they marched past. Local residents strongly objected to this and so the name was changed to coincide with where the fiercest fighting was taking place – Belgium.

The George

Overlooking Holyport's spacious green and adjacent to rows of pretty cottages and houses, the George's setting is certainly impressive. Until the 1980s this 400-year-old Grade II listed pub was also the venue for the village butcher. He owned the George, cleverly ensuring that his customers had to pass from one premises to the other to get what they wanted. The pub was refurbished in 2002 and its smart interior incorporates many of the traditional features associated with the licence trade. Food is served every day and includes omelettes, burgers, grilled plaice, beer-battered cod, breaded scampi, chilli con carne and steak and kidney pie. There are also jacket potatoes, sandwiches and baguettes. On Sunday traditional roast only is available. Children are allowed inside if eating. Large groups are asked to book. Telephone: 01628 628317.

The Walk

① From the pub turn right and cross the village green, keeping the war memorial and telephone box over on the left. Avoid Holyport Street and turn right by the pond into Moneyrow Green, signposted 'Holyport Memorial Hall'. Pass a bus stop and a house on the right called Longchase. Just beyond it swing left into Langworthy Lane and pass several attractive Georgian-style houses.

② Walk along to a path on the right, immediately beyond a house called Budds Oak. Follow the path between panel fencing, which soon gives way to hedges, with glimpses of fields here and there. Avoid a path on the right and disregard a path running off to the left a little further on. You may have to stop on occasions to let horses pass – this is a bridleway so walkers share it with cyclists and horseriders. Keep to the main path and eventually you reach the road by a line of houses.

③ Turn left and pass Amys Cottage and Rustlers View. Walk along to the last house on the left and head diagonally across the field, following the footpath. Make for a waymark and stile in the corner, cross a footbridge and head obliquely left in the field. A row of houses can be seen over to the right. Look for a pair of double galvanised gates and a stile just to the right of them.

④ Join a track and turn left, cutting

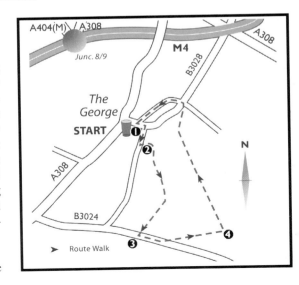

The return leg

between trees and hedgerows. There are very pleasant views over level farmland, with wooded country in the distance. Pass a footpath on the left and a stile and path on the right. Make for the houses of Holyport and when you reach the road, turn right. Pass Lynden Barn on the left and Langworthy End on the right and when you reach a T-junction, cross over to a byway. Follow it to Holyport Street and walk between picturesque houses and cottages. Pass the Belgian Arms on the left and return to the village green.

PLACES OF INTEREST NEARBY

Dorney Court, near Windsor, is a Grade I listed house characterised by a jumble of timber-framed gables. The large carved stone pineapple standing in the corner of the Great Hall commemorates the first pineapple to be grown in England. The story suggests that the top of a pineapple, imported from Barbados, was sliced off at a dinner in the City of London and given to the Earl of Castlemaine's gardener to plant at Dorney Court. The pineapple was subsequently presented to Charles II in 1661. Telephone: 01628 604638.

Hurley
The Dewdrop Inn

| MAP: OS EXPLORER 172 (GR 823815) | WALK 4 | DISTANCE: 4 MILES |

DIRECTIONS TO START: TAKE THE A4130 MAIDENHEAD TO HENLEY ROAD AND FOLLOW IT TO THE WEST OF HURLEY. TURN INTO HONEY LANE AND FOLLOW IT PAST SOME FARM OUTBUILDINGS. WHEN THE ROAD BENDS LEFT UNDER SOME TREES, TURN RIGHT AND RIGHT AGAIN TO THE PUB.
PARKING: THE CAR PARK AT THE DEWDROP INN IS THE MOST SUITABLE PLACE TO LEAVE A CAR.

Parts of this charming walk are under cover of trees – an attraction for naturalists and country walkers. It is hard to believe that Reading, Slough and Bracknell are close by. In places, the surroundings are so quiet and peaceful that you could be forgiven for thinking you are in the depths of Scotland or the wilds of Northumbria. The focal point of the walk is Hall Place, midway round the route. The house is Georgian and, until the Second World War, it was owned by the Clayton East family. Sold to the Ministry of Agriculture, Hall Place and part of the estate were acquired by Berkshire County Council in 1949 for the Berkshire Institute of Agriculture, later the Berkshire College of Agriculture. Rights of way running across the estate enable walkers to see the buildings at close quarters and get a feel for what goes on here.

The Dewdrop Inn

Surely one of Berkshire's most secluded pubs, the Dewdrop Inn was built as an ale house for forestry workers about 300 years ago. The setting has changed little since then. The pub is still buried deep in the heart of extensive woodland, reached only by a narrow winding lane, though the interior is more 21st century. Until 1996 the Dewdrop was run by a man whose love of golf and cricket was reflected by the many prints and photographs of sporting scenes which adorned the walls. Now under new management, the pub has been extensively refurbished, including the installation of a well equipped kitchen to meet the demands of its many customers. There is a good and appetising choice of bar food including ploughman's lunches, sandwiches and baguettes. There are also minute steaks, jumbo sausages, jacket potatoes, several vegetarian dishes and a choice of home-made specials. The Dewdrop offers a barbecue in summer but no food in the bar on Sunday evening throughout the year. Real ales include a seasonal beer. Telephone: 01628 824327.

The Walk

① Turn left out of the Dewdrop and then right at the junction. Continue ahead at a 'private' sign and follow the path to a waymarked junction. Turn left here and go up through the trees. Pass over a cross track and keep left at the fork. Ahead is the entrance to Clifton, an isolated house. Turn left here and follow the drive down through the woods. As it eventually sweeps to the right, go straight on to the road.

② Keep right and, when the road begins to curve to the right, look for a footpath branching left through the trees. Cross two stiles and skirt a fence and stream. Follow the path over a track by a gate and keep ahead towards houses. Cross two stiles to the road and look for two paths opposite.

③ Take the left-hand path and cut through the wood to Furze Cottage. Turn left at the road and walk along to the Crown pub on the left. Cross over into Hall Place Lane, keeping left at the entrance to Lane End House. Take the path to a gate and cross the field to an avenue of trees. Head towards Hall Place and swing right in front of the house.

④ Follow the drive to reach the vet's and veer half left just beyond it at the waymark. Once clear of the enclosures,

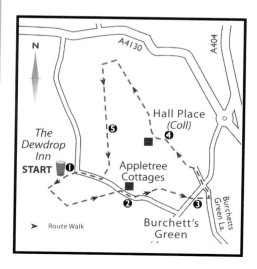

17

Hall Place

pass between trees and bushes to a crossroads. Keep left at the fork just beyond it and follow the clear track towards woodland. Make for a galvanised gate and take the path to the far end of the wood, swinging left to follow the fence. On reaching a pair of gates and a waymark, turn left and cut back through the wood. Make for another gate and then continue ahead between fields, towards Ashley Hill.

⑤ Cross two tracks and go through a gate, crossing the field to another gate. Follow the waymarked path through a belt of trees to the next gate and continue along the field edge. Pass a house and cross a stile out to the road. Turn right, go straight on at the bend and return to the inn.

PLACES OF INTEREST NEARBY

Littlewick Green, just off the A4, is one of Berkshire's prettiest villages. With its spacious green and picturesque cottages, it draws many visitors. You may even recognise it from a recent episode of the television series *Midsomer Murders*. At the south-east corner of the green lies a house called Red Roofs, now a theatre school. This was once the home of Ivor Novello (1893-1951), one of Britain's most prolific playwrights and composers and a contemporary of Noel Coward.

Aston
The Flower Pot

DIRECTIONS TO START: ASTON IS ABOUT 1 MILE NORTH OF THE A4130, ABOUT 2 MILES EAST OF HENLEY-ON-THAMES. **PARKING:** THERE IS ROOM TO PARK OPPOSITE THE PUB. PERMISSION HAS BEEN GIVEN BY THE LANDLORD FOR CUSTOMERS UNDERTAKING THIS WALK TO PARK HERE.

One of the most colourful stretches of the Thames is between Windsor and Reading, and some of the loveliest views of this most famous of rivers are enjoyed on this classic country walk. Stroll upstream to Temple Island in the depths of winter and the scene is likely to be calm and unhurried. Go back there in mid-summer, however, and it's a completely different picture. The little island, easily identified by its elegant Georgian folly around which sway alders and willows, birches and poplars, marks the official starting point for the annual Henley Regatta races held at the beginning of July. The course is 1 mile and 450 yards long and the event, an integral part of the British social calendar, dates back to 1839.

Cross broad green meadows, set against a glorious backdrop of hills and beechwoods, and keep an eye out for Hambleden Mill, originally driven by a water turbine, and Greenlands, a large white house built in 1853 for W. H. Smith.

The Flower Pot

A delightfully unspoilt pub, the late 19th-century Flower Pot still has a Victorian feel about it, evoking images of Jerome K Jerome's *Three Men in a Boat*. The inn was built to cater for 'boating parties and fishermen' – as the legend on the outside wall advertises. Inside, as well as wood-panelled walls with glass cases containing stuffed pike, you'll find a good choice of food, including pizza with chips and salad, honey roast ham, egg and chips, beefburger in a bun, half a roast chicken, ploughman's lunches, chicken and lamb balti, plaice with chips and peas, home-made moussaka, jumbo sausages and chilli con carne. The traditional ales are Brakspear's, and there is bed and breakfast accommodation and a popular beer garden with good views over the Thames Valley. Telephone: 01491 574721.

The Walk

① On leaving the pub turn left into Ferry Lane and pass a flint cottage. Walk out of Aston and follow the narrow lane between fields and light woodland. When you reach the water's edge at the site of the old ferry crossing, you have no choice but to turn left over a footbridge and through a kissing gate to join the towpath.

② Follow the Thames Path upstream, with the river on your right, crossing a tree-ringed meadow. Soon Hambleden Mill is glimpsed over on the opposite bank as you approach the weir and lock.

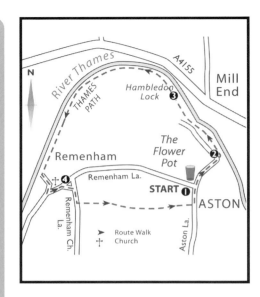

Go through a gate and join a tarmac track with the Thames hard by you on the right. There is now an even better view of the mill. Make for Hambleden Lock and look for a plaque on the left, which commemorates the official opening of a new lock by John Gummer, MP, Secretary of State for the Environment, in May 1994.

③ Pass through another kissing gate and return to the towpath. Note the impressive façade of Greenlands over on the far bank of the river and ahead now is Temple Island. Go through the next gate and continue towards Henley, crossing extensive meadows to reach some houses. Veer away from the river at this point and pass through a kissing gate, heading towards Remenham. Follow the path between brick and flint walls and pass Remenham Farmhouse on the right. At the church of St Nicholas turn left and follow the road to a fork.

The River Thames at Temple Island

④ Keep right and go up the steep slope. When the road levels out, walk along to a path junction. Turn left here and follow the track between fields. When, eventually, it curves to the left and begins to descend go straight on. Skirt a field and pass alongside laurel bushes. Make for a fence, with a large house visible on the left. Cross a stile and follow the path down to the road by Highway Cottage. Turn left and return to the Flower Pot.

PLACES OF INTEREST NEARBY

Henley-on-Thames – why not make a whole day of it and go on to visit this lovely riverside town, just a short drive from Aston? The central position of its parish church and the rectilinear layout of the town, which can still be traced today, are remnants of medieval planning. There are a number of local attractions and plenty of pubs, restaurants and cafés. Call the Tourist Information Centre on 01491 578034.

Crazies Hill
The Horns

MAP: OS EXPLORER 171 (GR 799808)	WALK 6	DISTANCE: $2^3/_4$ MILES

DIRECTIONS TO START: FROM HENLEY-ON-THAMES FOLLOW THE A4130 TOWARDS MAIDENHEAD. AT THE TOP OF REMENHAM HILL IS A TURNING FOR COCKPOLE GREEN AND CRAZIES HILL. TAKE THE TURNING AND FOLLOW THE ROAD UNTIL YOU REACH THE THIRD TURNING ON THE RIGHT. THE INN IS A SHORT DISTANCE ALONG THE LANE ON THE RIGHT. FROM MAIDENHEAD HEAD WEST ON THE A4 TO KNOWL HILL, THEN FOLLOW THE SIGNS FOR WARREN ROW AND CRAZIES HILL. **PARKING:** THERE IS PLENTY OF ROOM TO PARK AT THE INN.

Escape the noisy and intrusive world of motorways, dual carriageways and general traffic congestion and make for the peace and quiet of Bowsey Hill near Wargrave for this very attractive pub stroll. Much of the walk is beneath a canopy of dense woodland on the upper slopes of the Thames Valley – a perfect place for solitude and natural beauty. Only when you return to Crazies Hill, one of Berkshire's sleepier hamlets, are there signs of civilisation. Apparently, buttercups were once a common sight in this area and 'crazies' is a charming old country name for them. In the 1960s, Crazies Hill was the home of David Greig, a butcher who began a famous supermarket chain. His home was used as a training college.

The Horns

From the outside the Horns looks more like a cottage than an inn. It is a quaint old timber-framed building, which is thought to have been a Tudor hunting lodge in the days when Windsor Forest covered an extensive area of Berkshire, Hampshire and Surrey. Adjoining the bar is a 200-year-old barn which has been converted into a restaurant. Tastefully refurbished, these days the Horns is a popular dining pub, where customers can relax in one of three interconnecting rooms characterised by pine tables, exposed beams and open fires. Dishes on the daily-changing blackboard menus are likely to be roast guinea fowl with smoked bacon and herb gravy, chargrilled tuna steak, whole rainbow trout with lemon and coriander butter and roasted almonds, and rack of lamb with garlic and mint gravy. There is also a choice of baguettes and a range of puddings. At the rear of the pub is a pleasant garden where you can relax on a summer's day. Telephone: 01189 401416.

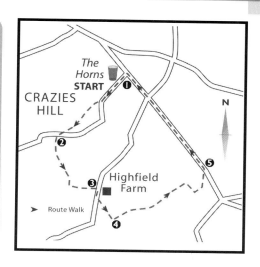

The Walk

① From the pub turn right and walk along to Crazies Hill Church of England primary school. Avoid a footpath and pass Crazies Hall on the right. Immediately beyond it, opposite the village hall, is a footpath on the right. Take the path and follow it between panel fencing and over a stretch of boardwalk. Further on, the path cuts through a tongue of woodland, with views over tree-ringed fields, before reaching the road.

② Turn right by a sign – 'unsuitable for motor vehicles' – and avoid the bridleway on the right. Follow the road for a few paces, then turn left at the footpath sign. Pick your way between the trees, several of them bearing white arrows to help guide you. Keep to the left of a bungalow, skirt its garden and make for a stile. Continue ahead in the field, with hedge and woodland on the left. Make for a gate and stile in the corner and keep ahead through a smattering of oak trees. Once clear of them, follow the path alongside a hedge to reach a waymark. Swing left here and follow the track to the road, with the buildings of Highfield Farm seen opposite.

③ Cross a stile and turn right, keeping the farm on your left. Pass a sign for Spring Meadows Business Centre and turn left at the footpath sign. Veer immediately right at this point and follow the path diagonally across the field towards woodland. Pass between two oak trees and on reaching a junction of paths, turn left.

Bowsey Hill

Continue ahead, with fields seen in the distance through the trees. Swing right at a gateway and follow the path through the wood to a stile. Turn left alongside a bungalow, by a bridleway sign, and go up the hill, following the track between properties.

⑤ Keep left at the junction at the top, pass alongside some sheds and timber barns and drop down between beech trees. Fields are soon glimpsed either side of the track between the trees and hedgerows. On reaching a crossroads, go straight over towards Crazies Hill. Turn left at the next junction and return to the inn.

④ Follow the sometimes muddy path through the sprawling woodland of Bowsey Hill, cutting between banks of bracken, brambles and vegetation. Eventually the path forks. Keep right here and pass over a path crossroads.

PLACES OF INTEREST NEARBY

Wargrave – this riverside village is usually quiet during the week, but often busy with visitors and boating enthusiasts at the weekend, especially in the summer. The village is distinctly Edwardian in appearance but its origins date back many centuries. The church among the trees dates from the First World War, replacing an earlier building that, except for the Norman tower, was destroyed by fire on Whit Sunday, 1914.

Waltham St Lawrence
The Bell

DIRECTIONS TO START: TAKE THE B3024 WINDSOR TO TWYFORD ROAD AND TURN INTO THE MAIN STREET OF WALTHAM ST LAWRENCE. THE INN IS A FEW YARDS FROM THE CHURCH. **PARKING:** THE PUB HAS A CAR PARK. IF BUSY, USE THE ROAD AT THE FRONT, WHERE THERE ARE LIMITED SPACES.

Waltham St Lawrence is one of those wonderful English villages that has the stamp of history all over it. During the Civil War there were village battles over respective allegiances to the Royalists and Parliamentarians. The churchyard is where the 18th-century publisher John Newbery is buried. He published the works of a number of great writers, including Dr Johnson.

Beyond the village the walk cuts across farmland to reach graceful Shottesbrooke Park, a prime example of classic English parkland. There was once a village here, but it fell victim to the Black Death soon after the church of St John the Baptist was built. According to legend, the church architect fell to his death from the top of the spire while attempting to repair the weather vane. Allegedly, he was buried where he fell and now lies under a flat stone near the door.

The Bell

One of Berkshire's oldest pubs, the Bell dates from the 14th century. During the Civil War, a small chamber enabled Parliamentarians to beat a hasty retreat through the pub's back entrance when Royalists were approaching. Built as a private house, the Bell passed to the village of Waltham St Lawrence in the 17th century and since those days it has been leased by the landlord. The rent goes to local charities. Fine old timber beams and some Jacobean panelling characterise the interior of the pub and just over the road is a pound where animals were once tethered. The bars and adjacent dining room can cater for large parties, though it is preferable to book. Food is available every session except Sunday evening and includes a good range of home-cooked daily specials and snacks. A traditional Sunday roast also forms part of the menu throughout the year. Main courses include bangers and mash, chicken tikka and fresh fish. Telephone: 01189 341788.

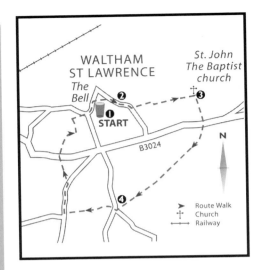

The Walk

① From the pub turn right towards the parish church and veer right into Halls Lane. Follow it between houses and then branch right at the footpath, following it between trees and gardens. Cross a drive and continue on the path to the road.

② Turn right and pass Halls Farm. The spire of the church at Shottesbrooke Park can be seen between the trees as you follow the lane. Walk along to a path junction and turn left, crossing a stile. Skirt the field alongside a fence and wall and head for some trees. Continue along the field boundary; over to the left in the distance are Bowsey Hill and Knowl Hill. Walk along to a stile and gate in the right boundary. Cross the tree-ringed field by keeping to the left edge and go through a brick arch. Keep ahead between sturdy buttressed brick walls. Pass through a second arch to reach the church.

③ Turn right just beyond it and follow the drive for a few yards to a sign for the Landmark Trust. Keep ahead at the waymark, parallel with the drive, and

PLACES OF INTEREST NEARBY

The **Berkshire Museum of Aviation** in Mohawk Way at Woodley is well worth a visit. The museum is dedicated to the contribution the county has made to flying. A Second World War hangar has been moved here from the old Woodley airfield and there are various aircraft representing Berkshire's aviation history of the last 60 years or so. Telephone: 01189 448089.

St John the Baptist church, Shottesbrooke Park

ahead to a gate, cross a field to a stile and join a path on a bend. Go straight on and eventually you reach the road.

④ Turn right, then almost immediately left at the junction. Cross the road by the 'Shurlock Row' sign and take the path, following it to the left of some houses. Go through three kissing gates, cross a pasture to some wooden panel fencing and exit to the road at the next gate. Turn right and make for a kissing gate at the point where the road curves right. Cross the field to a line of houses at the road and make for a gate and path opposite. Make for the trees ahead in the far boundary where you'll find a kissing gate. Keep to the right edge of the field and, on

cross the parkland. Make for a stile and two gates before exiting to the road. Cross over to a footpath and pass alongside a pair of semi-detached houses. Follow the path reaching a waymark, turn left towards panel fencing and a bungalow. Turn right at a junction of paths and head for the road. Turn right and return to the inn.

Wokingham
The Metropolitan

| MAP: OS EXPLORER 159 (GR 813687) | WALK 8 | DISTANCE: 3 MILES |

DIRECTIONS TO START: FROM EAST OR WEST FOLLOW THE M4 AND THEN TAKE THE A329M (JUNCTION 10) FOR WOKINGHAM. MAKE FOR THE TOWN CENTRE, KEEP RIGHT AT THE SHIP INN INTO WILTSHIRE ROAD, THEN TURN LEFT BY ALL SAINTS CHURCH INTO ROSE STREET. THE METROPOLITAN IS ON THE RIGHT. **PARKING:** THERE IS A SMALL CAR PARK AT THE REAR OF THE INN.

History and architecture are the twin themes on this fascinating stroll, which begins as a heritage trail around Wokingham and then turns its back on the noise and bustle of the town, heading for pretty countryside to the south. To appreciate Wokingham's hidden corners and handsome buildings fully, get hold of a good street map and an informative booklet on this classic market town. Founded in the 13th century by the Norman-French Bishop Roger le Poore, Wokingham was granted a charter by Queen Elizabeth in 1583. Until the 19th century the town developed at a slow pace, but in recent years it has grown enormously, its rapid expansion a direct result of the nearby M4 and Wokingham's rail link to London. The walk's halfway point is represented by Lucas Hospital, the splendid Grade I listed almshouses built in 1665 by Henry Lucas for sixteen poor bachelors.

The Metropolitan

The Grade II 16th-century Metropolitan is one of the oldest pubs in Wokingham. It prides itself on being a traditional, old-world pub with a very friendly and welcoming atmosphere. Everyone feels safe and once inside it is like stepping back to an age when town hostelries were cosy and intimate and good conversation was the order of the day. There are always four home-cooked daily specials and among the typical dishes on offer are spaghetti bolognese, fresh fish, liver and bacon and a traditional roast. Omelettes, baguettes, sandwiches and soup are always available. Food is served every lunchtime but not in the evening. Dogs are permitted inside but children are restricted to the patio garden at the rear. The Metropolitan is open all day. Telephone: 01189 784466.

The Walk

① Turn right on leaving the pub and walk along Rose Street, the finest example in Berkshire of a medieval 'enclosed' street. The street is wide at one end and narrow at the other. One of its more famous residents was James 'Sooty' Seaward, who was the inspiration for Tom, the chimney sweep, the central character in Charles Kingsley's classic *The Water Babies*, published in 1863. Veer left into the Market Place and, with the 19th-century town hall on your right, walk down Denmark Street. Pass the Wokingham Memorial Clinic and keep right at the Dukes Head pub. Walk to the roundabout, cross Kendrick Close and follow Finchampstead Road. Pass under

PLACES OF INTEREST NEARBY

The **Tudor House**, at the far end of Broad Street and dating back to the mid-16th century, is one of Wokingham's most historic and attractive buildings. The front was partly altered in the early 20th century by incorporating timbers from a nearby dismantled mansion. Until the end of the First World War the building housed a school.

the railway and take the footpath on the left at the next roundabout.

② Head for a gate, veer right by some loose-boxes and follow a fenced track. Make for a line of houses and continue to Lucas Hospital. Retrace your steps towards the loose-boxes and on reaching some paddocks take the path on the right to the next boundary. The outskirts of Wokingham are visible up ahead on the hillside. Cross the next field to a footbridge and then go up the slope, passing under power lines to enter an area of woodland. The ground here can be wet

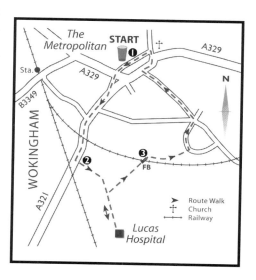

Lucas Hospital

and boggy. Soon you come to a footbridge over the railway line.

③ Cross the bridge and veer right on the opposite side, following Gypsy Lane. Pass Southfields School, cross Erica Drive and continue to the next main junction. Cross Murdoch Road and follow Easthampstead Road towards the town centre. Turn right at the T-junction and walk along to the Ship Inn. Keep to the left of the Ship Inn, turn right shortly into Cross Street and follow it to Rose Street. Turn left and the Metropolitan is on the right.

Barkham
The Bull

| MAP: OS EXPLORER 159 (GR 779668) | WALK 9 | DISTANCE: 2¼ MILES |

DIRECTIONS TO START: FOLLOW THE B3349 BETWEEN WOKINGHAM AND ARBORFIELD CROSS. THE BULL IS ON THE CORNER OF THE ROAD TO BARKHAM CHURCH. **PARKING:** THERE IS A CAR PARK AT THE REAR OF THE BULL. AVOID PARKING ON THE 3349.

Glance at a map of Berkshire and you'll see that squeezed between Reading and Wokingham is a surprisingly secluded area of wooded countryside – once part of Windsor Forest. In a hectic, bustling world, this is a haven for walkers, strollers and horseriders. Quiet paths and tracks pick their way between the trees, giving the impression you are miles from civilisation and deep in the heart of the forest. In fact, you are never more than a few hundred yards from a busy road, a residential development or a golf course – a familiar part of the Berkshire landscape. Bearwood Golf Club lies adjacent to a large estate of the same name, once the home of the Walter family who founded *The Times* in the late 18th century. The woods are known for junipers, cedars and rhododendrons and the 40-acre lake in the grounds was where the fourth John Walter died trying to rescue his brother.

The Bull

This historic pub is known as the 'Bull at Barkham', so as not to confuse it with the Bull at nearby Arborfield. It used to be a working forge, part of which can be still be seen in the restaurant. Children and dogs are welcome inside and a cosy log fire creates a welcoming atmosphere in winter. Expect a good range of home-made dishes on the menu, including steak and ale pie, liver and bacon, bangers and mash, curry, chilli con carne, scampi, cod and various specials. There are soup, ploughman's lunches and, at lunchtime, a choice of baguettes. No bookings apart from large groups. Relax in the beer garden on a summer's day – an ideal venue following a short stroll in the neighbouring countryside. Telephone: 01189 760324.

A leafy track

② On reaching a fork, keep right and climb gently to a junction. Keep right here and pass a bungalow on the right. Follow the track round to the right and soon its surface graduates to tarmac. Cut between properties to reach the road.

The Walk

① From the Bull car park turn left, then right to join the B3349 road. Pass Bailiff's Cottage on the right and a few paces beyond it branch left to leave the busy road at a bridleway. Cross a private drive and continue ahead on the bridle track. Note the contrast between the traffic on the B3349 and the peace and tranquillity of the countryside. The track narrows to a path further on and passes some gates on the left and right.

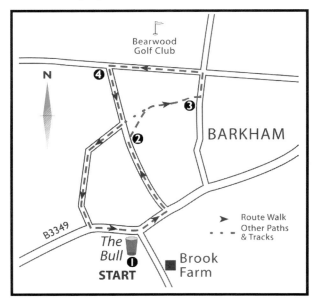

Secluded countryside near Barkham

③ Turn left and go up the hill to a crossroads. On the right is Sandy Lane. Bear left into Coombes Lane and pass Alexion House on the left. Beyond it the lane becomes an unmade track. On the right you can see the fairways of Bearwood Golf Club. Continue ahead through the woodland.

④ Turn left at the next bridleway and follow the path along the edge of the wood. Further on the path plunges deeper into the wood. Take the first bridleway on the right and pass a footpath on the right. When the path forks in front of you, keep

> ### PLACES OF INTEREST NEARBY
> **California Country Park** is a popular attraction with families. The park includes many different species of tree, a lake, dragonfly pond, fishing, children's play equipment and an information centre. Telephone: 01189 730028.

left and stay as close as you can to the field on the left. Descend quite steeply and pass alongside wooden panel fencing to reach Barkham's Old Rectory. Continue ahead along the drive to the road and turn left. Follow the pavement back to the Bull.

Finchampstead
The Queen's Oak

MAP: OS EXPLORER 159 (GR 793638)

WALK 10

DISTANCE: 5 MILES

DIRECTIONS TO START: FINCHAMPSTEAD LIES BETWEEN THE A321 AND THE A327, ABOUT 7 MILES SOUTH OF READING. IN THE VILLAGE, TAKE THE ROAD SIGNPOSTED 'TO THE CHURCH'. THE INN CAN BE SEEN AS YOU REACH THE GREEN. **PARKING:** THERE IS A CAR PARK AT THE QUEEN'S OAK AND SOME SPACES ELSEWHERE IN THE VILLAGE.

History is a strong theme on this delightful walk in the countryside around Finchampstead. The church, a few paces from the start, was built on the site of an ancient earthwork and is Norman in origin. Inside is a plaque in memory of General Sir John Watson, who won the Victoria Cross at the siege of Lucknow. As you head back into Finchampstead on the return leg, look for a wooden sign beside the route. According to some sources, it was here, in November 1501, that Henry VII and his sons, Arthur and Henry, rode to meet Catherine of Aragon following her arrival from Spain. The King and the two princes had been hunting in the area when they learnt that Catherine had reached Henry's hunting lodge at Dogmersfield. Ten days later, on 14th November, Catherine and Arthur were married in St Paul's Cathedral. He was just 15 and she was almost 16.

The Queen's Oak

The Queen's Oak occupies a charming setting well away from busy roads and the more built-up parts of Finchampstead. Just across the road is a pretty green with a memorial plaque marking Queen Victoria's Diamond Jubilee in 1897. An oak tree, which gave the inn its name, was planted here ten years earlier to celebrate the 50th year of her reign. At the side of the pub is a large enclosed garden, pleasantly shaded by trees, while inside are a bar and dining area where quality, home-cooked food is served. The menu offers everything from sandwiches and ploughman's lunches to steak and ale pie and liver and bacon. One additional service will appeal especially to ramblers. By calling the pub before the walk, you can book a table and choose what you want to eat so that it is ready on your return. Telephone: 01189 734855.

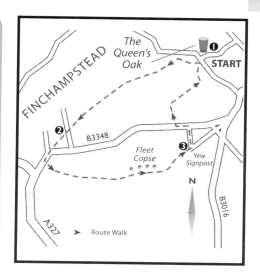

The Walk

① From the pub turn right towards the church, following the footpath sign. Keep right as the lane forks and soon it dwindles to a stony track, descending through a wooded tunnel. Pass the entrance to Manor Beacon, cross the next road and follow the path between bracken and hedges. Make for a waymarked junction of paths and continue ahead, with several gates on the right. Follow the clear path as it cuts between fields and through woodland. Keep alongside a hedgerow to a stile and out onto a lane.

② Cross over to a kissing gate and skirt the field, keeping the fence on your immediate right. Make for a gate ahead, pass between trees to the road and turn right. Bear left at the sign for Vann House and follow the track to Fleethill Farm. Keep to the left of the outbuildings, head for a stile and continue alongside the woodland edge to a stile in the field corner. Turn left after a few paces and follow the path between trees, joining a drive on the edge of Finchampstead.

③ Pass a left turning and just beyond it is the wooden signpost made from pieces of yew. Retrace your steps for a few yards and

PLACES OF INTEREST NEARBY

Finchampstead Ridges is close to the starting point of this walk. It comprises 60 acres of superb woodland, including a heather ridge, and is owned by the National Trust. There is an extensive network of paths and much to interest the naturalist and ornithologist. Spotted flycatchers and siskins are among the many species to be found here.

Strolling back to Finchampstead

turn right, passing alongside a fence and beneath the boughs of holly trees. Turn left by the garage and walk along to a drive on the right leading to Rectory Farm. Follow it to a stile and path to the right of the main gate, swing right after about 60 yards and cut between paddocks. Cross the next stile, followed by a footbridge, turn left, then right. Swing left at the next junction and head for Finchampstead church. Walk through the churchyard and return to the Queen's Oak.

Gardeners Green
The Crooked Billet

MAP: OS EXPLORER 159 (GR 826668)

WALK 11

DISTANCE: 2 MILES

DIRECTIONS TO START: FROM WOKINGHAM'S INNER RING ROAD MAKE FOR EASTHAMPSTEAD ROAD. TURN RIGHT INTO HEATHLANDS ROAD AND THEN LEFT INTO HONEY HILL. THE INN IS ON THE LEFT. **PARKING:** THERE IS A SPACIOUS CAR PARK AT THE SIDE OF THE PUB.

Squeezed between Wokingham, Bracknell and Crowthorne lies a delightfully unspoiled tract of classic countryside. This was once part of the great Windsor Forest, which covered much of east Berkshire. Pockets of the forest survive today. Close to the start of this easy, undemanding walk there are distant glimpses of Ludgrove School, one of Britain's best-known prep schools. Ludgrove began life as Wixenford School in 1892 and moved to its present 130-acre site in 1937. A number of notable public figures have attended Ludgrove over the years – among them Sir Alec Douglas Home, the Duke of Devonshire and, of course, the two royal princes, William and Harry. The son of British film actress Glynis Johns was also a pupil here. If you study the map before setting out, you might be inspired to extend the route and explore Bramshill Forest – a peaceful world of pine woods where the only sound is the soothing sigh of the breeze in the trees.

The Crooked Billet

The Crooked Billet's weatherboarded façade is one among many attractive features to be found at this popular country pub. The interior is quaint and welcoming, with lots of beams, a cosy fireplace with a copper hood and an interesting illustrated history of bicycles and tricycles on the wall. The toilets are unusually named 'Bonnets' and 'Tophats'! Adjoining the bar is an intimate non-smoking restaurant for which booking is advisable. Dishes on the menu are fresh and home produced and the choice is comprehensive. Starters include Stilton and walnut salad and pan-fried tiger prawns, while main courses are likely to be grilled salmon, minted lamb cutlets, chicken curry, liver and bacon, chilli con carne and bangers and mash. Sandwiches and baguettes are also on offer. No food is served on Sunday evening. Well-behaved dogs are allowed and children under 14 are permitted in the restaurant only. A beer garden and play area also feature among the attractions. Telephone: 01189 780438.

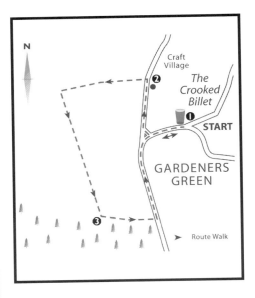

The Walk

① From the inn turn right and walk along Honey Hill to the junction with Heathlands Road. Turn right and cut between trees and houses. Pass the drive to Holme Grange Farm and then the entrance to Holme Grange Craft Village, where there are a number of shops.

② Continue on the road for about 70

Bramshill Forest

The grounds of Ludgrove School

yards and then turn left at the footpath sign. Walk along to Grays Farm, pass the farm outbuildings on the right and follow the track to the left of some greenhouses. Ludgrove School can be seen now, over to the right among the trees. On reaching a T-junction, opposite a private property sign, turn left and cut through a fruit growing area, heading south towards woodland. Follow the path to the edge of the trees.

③ Go through a gate in the deer fence and then turn immediately left. Keep to the path as it runs through the woodland and when you reach the road, turn left.

PLACES OF INTEREST NEARBY

The **Look Out Discovery Park**, at nearby Nine Mile Ride, is situated in 2,600 acres of woodland. There is much to do, including walks and nature trails, a gift shop, picnic area, Tourist Information Centre, coffee shop, children's events and exhibitions. The site also has plenty of free car parking. Telephone: 01344 868222.

Pass a farm and follow the road as it curves right. Take the next right turning and walk back along Honey Hill to the Crooked Billet.

Farley Hill
The Fox and Hounds

DIRECTIONS TO START: FROM READING FOLLOW THE A327 TO ARBORFIELD. CONTINUE TOWARDS EVERSLEY AND THEN TURN RIGHT FOR FARLEY HILL. THE PUB IS ON THE LEFT, ON A BEND.
PARKING: THERE IS ROOM TO PARK AT THE FRONT OF THE PUB AND IN THE ROAD.

Farley Hill lies to the south of Reading in a rural district which was once part of Windsor Forest. The surrounding countryside, still surprisingly green and unspoiled, cries out to be discovered and anyone exploring it on foot soon comes to appreciate its varied delights. Part of this tranquil stroll follows a section of the 19-mile Blackwater Valley Path, a waymarked recreational route running the entire length of the valley, mostly alongside the river, which flows serenely along Berkshire's southern boundary with Hampshire. While at Farley Hill have a look at the churchyard, which is peaceful and pleasantly shaded by trees. Look more closely and you'll see that there are no gravestones here, only neatly mown grass and thick foliage. The red-brick Victorian church stands on unconsecrated ground, so no burials are permitted. Across the road lies Farley Court, once the home of Charles Kingsley who wrote the children's classic *The Water Babies*. For many years Kingsley was the vicar of nearby Eversley church.

The Fox and Hounds

One of my favourite pubs in this part of Berkshire, the Fox and Hounds still has the feel of a traditional village local. According to the family who run the business, the pub is built on 200-year-old foundations, though the present building dates back only to the 1840s, when Morland chose this site for a hostelry. The bar is small and intimate with stone flooring and wood panelling. It's a great favourite of ramblers so if you call on spec don't be surprised to find it overrun with anorak and boot-clad figures tucking into scampi or steak and ale pie. The landlords are very flexible on food and cater for most tastes. The last time I was there they knocked up sausage and chips for me even though it didn't appear on the menu! There are the usual snacks – sandwiches and jacket potatoes, as well as a variety of other fare. It's a good idea to book in advance, especially if there is going to be a large gathering. That way you can choose what you want when you arrive, go off for a country stroll and then return to find the food waiting for you. On summer evenings, you can go one better by relaxing in the adjacent beer garden and enjoying the lovely view. The Fox and Hounds opens between 3.30 pm and 11 pm on Monday, Tuesday and Wednesday, and from 12 noon on Thursday, Friday, Saturday and Sunday. Food is available every day and there is a traditional roast on Sunday. Well-behaved children and dogs are welcome. Telephone: 01189 733266.

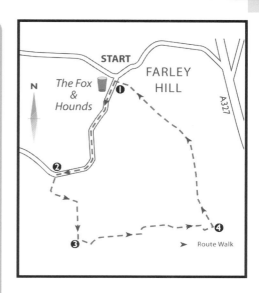

The Walk

① On leaving the Fox and Hounds, turn right into Jouldings Lane and follow it between trees and hedgerows. There are good views over the Blackwater Valley to the south. Pass Cheriton Farm and avoid a path on the left leading down to the edge of a lake. After prolonged spells of rain this stretch of the walk can be very wet and muddy underfoot. Swing left at the point where a byway branches off to the right.

② Head south, pass a footpath on the right and on reaching a timber-framed and red brick house, turn left to a stile. Follow the Blackwater Valley Path to the next stile and join an enclosed path alongside a tennis court. Walk along to the next stile, turn right and cross a paddock to a stile and footbridge over a stream by the River Blackwater. Go through the trees to the next stile and keep right in the next paddock to two stiles in the corner. Keep ahead alongside the river and then cross the field to a stile.

Walking in the Blackwater Valley

③ At the junction with the woodland path, turn left and cut through a tunnel of trees. Cross a stile by a gate and swing left and follow the path alongside Greenacres Farm on the left. Keep ahead through several bends and pass a house called Nettleberry. Further on is a picturesque timber-framed cottage and just beyond it is Forge House. Go round a right-hand bend and pass Lea Cottage on the left.

④ Turn left immediately past Lea Cottage and go through a gate to join a footpath. Keep Lea Cottage on the left and as you approach a field, turn left and skirt it. Make for a stile in the corner and continue through light woodland. Cross a footbridge to a stile and then cross the field by aiming slightly left, passing under

power lines. Head for the top-left corner, cross a stile and keep trees on your right. Turn left at a waymark, cross the field to the far boundary, turn right and follow the path up the bank to a private garden. Skirt it and then turn left to join a narrow path running between houses. On reaching the road, turn left and return to the pub.

PLACES OF INTEREST NEARBY

Swallowfield Park, owned by the Country Houses Association Ltd, is close to the route of the walk at Farley Hill and is open to the public on Wednesday and Thursday afternoons between May and September. The house is late 17th century and has the Blackwater running through its parkland. Telephone: 01189 883815.

Mortimer
The Horse and Groom

MAP: OS EXPLORER 159
(GR 655645)

WALK 13

DISTANCE: $3\frac{1}{4}$ MILES

DIRECTIONS TO START: COMING FROM READING, TAKE THE A33 BASINGSTOKE ROAD. JUST SOUTH OF JUNCTION 11 OF THE M4, TURN RIGHT, PASS THROUGH GRAZELEY AND MAKE FOR MORTIMER. THERE IS A RAILWAY STATION AT NEARBY STRATFIELD MORTIMER. **PARKING:** THERE IS A PUBLIC CAR PARK OPPOSITE THE HORSE AND GROOM.

Think of places like Aldermaston and Burghfield and your mind is perhaps filled with images of sinister-looking buildings, high perimeter fences and security men with dogs – MoD country. In their shadow, however, lies a delightfully wooded area of countryside where walkers can explore an intricate network of peaceful paths and tracks. This undiscovered corner of Berkshire, unknown to those who only travel this way by car, is perfect for rambling and I have chosen the sprawling village of Mortimer as the starting point for a very varied and enjoyable country stroll. Cutting across farmland and through dense woodland, this is an attractive walk in any season. Before you begin, have a look at the illustrated information boards in the car park opposite the Horse and Groom. They explain the history and management of two ponds here, as well as highlighting the wildlife associated with them.

The Horse and Groom

The Horse and Groom opened as a pub in 1860. It was originally next door, before that premises became a butcher's shop. A good menu is offered – everything from light snacks to substantial meals. Roast lamb, sausage, egg and chips, game pie, steak and ale pie, ham, egg and chips and scampi are among the popular dishes, while baguettes, sandwiches, burgers and soup feature among the lighter fare. There is also a children's menu and a traditional daily roast is served. Relax in the bar or the non-smoking dining area; alternatively, there is a large and very popular beer garden. The Horse and Groom is open all day from Wednesday to Sunday, and keeps 'normal' licensing hours the rest of the week, but no food on Monday. Large parties are asked to book. Well-behaved dogs are permitted inside. Telephone: 01189 332813.

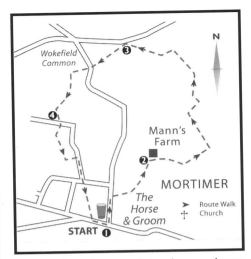

The Walk

① From the pub turn right and follow the main road towards the war memorial, turning left at the sign for Hammonds Heath. Walk along to the 30-mile per hour speed restriction sign and swing right, passing through the galvanised gate. Cut between trees and bracken to reach a junction. Merge with a path and continue ahead, avoiding a path on the right. Cross fields to the road by a farm and turn right.

② Look for a path on the left beyond the outbuildings, cross two footbridges into a field and turn immediately right. Follow the boundary to a stile and turn left. Make for a track at the top of the slope and turn right. Head for a stile on the left and follow the path down the field edge to a stile and footbridge in the corner. Cross over and follow the path up towards a line of trees. Make for a narrow lane and turn left.

On the route

A tranquil corner of Berkshire

③ On reaching the next junction, at Wokefield Common, swing left to follow a track running alongside Pound Green Cottage. Keep right at the fork just beyond it and take the clear path through the woods. Merge with a track and continue to the next road. Cross over and keep ahead on the bridleway. Turn left further on and follow the right of way between a house and its garden. The path descends, then climbs quite steeply. Keep ahead to a junction with a track and turn right, then left after a few paces.

④ On reaching a lane turn left and then bear right at a farmhouse to join a byway. Follow the path along the woodland edge before climbing between trees to a clearing amidst firs. Fir cones cover the

PLACES OF INTEREST NEARBY

Calleva Atrebatum, or Silchester as it is more usually known, provides a fascinating insight into the Roman occupation when this was the site of an important town. There is also a small museum worth visiting. Telephone the Tourist Information Centre on 01189 566226.

ground here. Swing left at this point and follow the path to the road. Turn right and walk along to the junction. Mortimer church can be seen across the playing fields. Cross over to a kissing gate opposite and then head diagonally left to a second gate. Keep to the left of the hard tennis court and return to the car park opposite the inn.

Aldermaston
The Butt Inn

<table>
<tr><td>MAP: OS EXPLORER 159
(GR 601668)</td><td>WALK 14</td><td>DISTANCE: 3 MILES</td></tr>
</table>

DIRECTIONS TO START: FOLLOW THE A4 WEST OF JUNCTION 12 OF THE M4 AT THEALE. TAKE THE A340 (SIGNPOSTED 'ALDERMASTON'), CROSS THE KENNET AND AVON CANAL AT ALDERMASTON WHARF AND THE BUTT IS ON THE RIGHT. **PARKING:** THE PUB HAS ITS OWN CAR PARK AT THE SIDE.

Drive along the A4 between Reading and Newbury and you glimpse some of Berkshire's grandest ancestral homes standing amid the lush pastures of the Kennet Valley. On its gentle, north-facing slopes is handsome Padworth House, one of the main features of this very pleasant canal-side stroll. Set in eleven acres and recalling the great days of weekend house parties and servants below stairs, the present house dates back to 1769. It was the home of Padworth's last squire, Major Darby-Griffith, who shot himself on Armistice Day 1932 because

he feared he was losing his sight. Since 1963 the house has been an international girls' school with its pupils representing 24 different nationalities. The Kennet and Avon Canal first opened in 1810 and was built to link Bristol and Reading, transporting timber, coal and flour among other products. The coming of the Great Western Railway eventually sounded the death knell on the canal and gradually it fell into disuse. But it was not entirely forgotten. Armies of enthusiasts spent years restoring the waterway and it was finally reopened by the Queen in 1990.

The Butt Inn

The Butt Inn at Aldermaston Wharf is the only pub in the village that is close to the Kennet and Avon Canal. Not surprisingly, it draws large numbers of cyclists, walkers and boating enthusiasts – especially during the warmer months. Tables and benches and various pot plants and hanging baskets give the front of the inn a bustling, colourful look and in summer, when the Butt is open all day at weekends, customers are attracted to the beer garden at the rear. Wooden floors and log fires enhance the atmosphere and appeal inside the pub, where you can relax in the bar area or the restaurant. Sandwiches, baguettes and jacket potatoes make up the snack menu, while lasagne, chilli con carne, chicken curry and smoked ham and mushroom tagliatelle feature among the main dishes. There are also several starters and a range of steak and fish dishes. Food is served every day and there is a traditional Sunday roast. Booking is preferable at weekends. Telephone: 01189 712129.

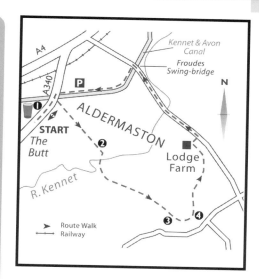

The Walk

① From the pub turn left and walk along the road towards Aldermaston Lock and the road bridge. Turn right immediately before it and keep right at the immediate fork. Pass some cottages and continue to the next footpath on the right.

② Follow the path between conifers and wooden panel fencing and then cross several footbridges over the River Kennet. Water plunges beneath you in a foaming, raging torrent and beyond the weirs you reach a stile. Cross the field to the next stile and a footbridge crossing a stream. Beyond the water aim diagonally left across the next field towards a line of trees. Pass under some power lines and cross another footbridge. In the next field head towards Padworth College, crossing a stile just to the right of a gate. Keep the fence on your left and go up the slope to the next stile. Ahead of you now are farm outbuildings.

PLACES OF INTEREST NEARBY

The Vyne at Sherborne St John, between Aldermaston and Basingstoke, is a fine country house whose features include a Tudor chapel with Renaissance glass and a Palladian staircase. Telephone: 01256 881337.

The Visitor Centre at Aldermaston Wharf offers canal information and sells gifts, souvenirs and refreshments. The towpath here is ideal for a family walk. For more details, telephone: 01189 712868.

The Kennet and Avon Canal at Aldermaston

your left. Cross the paddock and enter the churchyard of St John the Baptist. You can't fail to spot the ancient yew tree at the front. Make for the lychgate and war memorial and then veer left into the trees.

④ Cross the main drive to Padworth College, pass alongside a lake where herons are sometimes seen and follow the waymarked path through the grounds. Make for a kissing gate, cross into a field and continue with the fence on your left and your back to the college. Cross a stile and follow the drive down to the road. Turn left and walk along to the Kennet and Avon Canal. Turn left and join the footpath, following it along to a boatyard. Pass the canal visitor centre and make for the road bridge ahead. Turn left and return to the pub.

③ On approaching some stables, turn left and cross the stile, keeping a single storey building known as The Bothy on

Pangbourne
The Cross Keys

MAP: OS EXPLORER 159
(GR 633765)

WALK 15

DISTANCE: 3 MILES

DIRECTIONS TO START: PANGBOURNE LIES AT THE JUNCTION OF THE A329 READING ROAD AND THE A340, WHICH LEADS TO THE A4 AT THEALE AND JUNCTION 12 OF THE M4. THE CROSS KEYS IS ON THE A340, OPPOSITE THE CHURCH, IN THE CENTRE OF THE VILLAGE. PANGBOURNE IS ALSO ON THE MAIN LONDON TO OXFORD RAILWAY LINE AND THE STATION IS A SHORT WALK FROM THE PUB.
PARKING: THE CROSS KEYS DOES NOT HAVE A CAR PARK. HOWEVER, THERE IS A PUBLIC CAR PARK CLOSE BY ON THE OPPOSITE SIDE OF THE ROAD, NEAR THE RAILWAY BRIDGE.

'Pleasant house, hate Pangbourne, nothing happens,' wrote D. H. Lawrence in 1919 when he and his German wife, Frieda, rented a cottage in the village. At that time Pangbourne was especially fashionable with artists, writers and weekend anglers and, with the glorious Thames greatly enhancing its setting, the place soon gained a reputation as a highly desirable inland resort. One man whose love for Pangbourne and the river lasted a lifetime was the writer Kenneth Grahame, who first came to live in Berkshire when he was five. He moved to Pangbourne in 1924 and died here eight years later. This pretty riverside walk captures something of the spirit of his writing, journeying initially beside the Pang and then following the Thames upstream to Whitchurch Bridge.

The Cross Keys

The 16th-century Cross Keys, opposite the parish church, is one of Pangbourne's oldest buildings and certainly one of its quaintest. The pub's interior is charming, with a delightful jumble of rooms and classic low ceilings. At the rear is a most attractive patio with a gazebo where you can sit and relax by the trickling River Pang. A word of warning, however. If you're planning to visit the Cross Keys on a sunny Sunday in summer, get there as early as possible as the patio fills up very quickly. Traditional Sunday roast is a great favourite, but there are plenty of other dishes to tempt you. Expect the usual range of snacks and light meals, including soup of the day, steak baguette and BLT, a perennially popular choice. For something more substantial you might like to try pot roast shank of lamb, confit leg of duck, sea bass, trio of sausages or Stilton, beef and mushroom pie. The Cross Keys is open all day, with food available at lunchtime and in the evening. Telephone: 01189 843268.

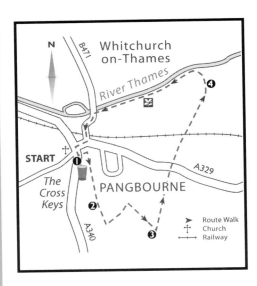

The Walk

① From the pub turn right to the mini-roundabout, then right again. Cross the Pang and turn right at the next main junction into The Moors. At the end of the drive continue ahead on a waymarked footpath. Pass alongside various houses and gardens and patches of scrub, then go through a tunnel of trees. Further on is a gate with a local map and an information board beside it. Beyond the gate the Pang sweeps in from the right.

② Follow the riverside path to a footbridge. Avoid it and turn sharp left at this point, crossing open meadowland to a stile in the far boundary. Once over it, keep alongside the hedge on the left and, as you approach a wartime pill-box, turn right at a path intersection and cross a footbridge. Head for another footbridge on the far side of the field and then look for a third bridge with white railings. Cross the bridge and the stile beyond it and then head across the field to the far boundary.

③ Exit to the road and turn left. Follow the lane between hedges and oak trees and walk along to the A329. Go diagonally right to the footpath by the sign for Purley Rise and follow the path north towards distant trees. Turn right at the next bridge and follow the concrete track as it bends left to run beneath the railway line. Once

The River Thames

through the arch, turn right to a stile and then follow the track along the left edge of the field, beside a rivulet. Pass double gates and a bridge on the left and continue on the path to a stile. Cross the next field to reach the river bank.

④ Turn left and follow the Thames Path upstream towards Pangbourne. Soon you reach Pangbourne Meadow and up ahead now is Whitchurch Bridge. As you approach it, begin to veer away from the river towards a car park. Keep left when you reach the road, pass beneath the railway line again and turn right at the next junction. Turn right at the mini-roundabout for the car park, or left for the Cross Keys.

PLACES OF INTEREST NEARBY

The **church of St James the Less**, with its square tower and battlements dominating the skyline, is opposite the Cross Keys. Kenneth Grahame's funeral took place here in July 1932 and was recorded in *The Times*. The writer lived next door at Church Cottage.

Streatley
The Bull

DIRECTIONS TO START: FOLLOW THE A329 BETWEEN READING AND WALLINGFORD TO REACH STREATLEY. COMING FROM NEWBURY, TAKE THE B4009. THE BULL LIES AT THE FOOT OF STREATLEY HILL, BY THE CROSSROADS IN THE CENTRE OF THE VILLAGE.
PARKING: USE THE BULL CAR PARK AT THE REAR OF THE PUB.

There are several climbs on this very attractive Thames Valley walk but the effort is rewarded by magnificent views over the river. Look out for an unusual feature as you cross the fairways at Streatley and Goring Golf Club. A bell at the side of the path enables you to alert nearby players and thus avoid possible injury. Simple but effective. Higher up, the path reaches the sunny glades and peaceful clearings of a plateau managed by the National Trust and known as The Holies. On this stretch of the walk you'll probably welcome the chance to pause, rest and relax after the earlier rigours. There are several seats here – one of them in memory of Berkshire writer and rambler Mick Tapp, who died in 1999 aged 60. Continue through the woodland and suddenly, as you emerge from the trees, you get a breathtaking view of the Thames snaking through the countryside far below. Both Streatley and adjacent Goring, nicknamed 'discreetly and boring' by locals, can be clearly seen from here.

The Bull

One of Berkshire's most historic pubs, the Bull was once a coaching inn for the Royal Mail coach to Oxford. Early in the 20th century, much of Streatley was owned by the famous Morrell brewing family. The main characters in Jerome K. Jerome's *Three Men in a Boat* visited the Bull, 'much to Montmorency's satisfaction', and the inn still boasts a post box and a wheel pump at the front. The pub has supplied fresh water for centuries and records indicate that during the great freeze of 1895 water was sold here for sixpence a bucket. The ancient yew in the garden supposedly marks the burial site of a nun and a monk executed in 1440 for misconduct, though the story was never proved. The pub's 15th-century interior is attractive and inviting with welcome fires adding to the cosy atmosphere in winter. The menu offers a wide selection of hearty dishes, daily specials, vegetarian meals and seafood specialities. Expect Bull Pie, medallions of pork, Cumberland sausage ring and scampi tails among other fare. Hand-pumped cask ales are also available. The Bull is open all day on Friday, Saturday and Sunday, and keeps 'normal' licensing hours the rest of the week. Telephone: 01491 872392.

The Walk

① From the pub car park turn left to begin climbing the hill. Swing right after a few paces to join a stony drive cutting between houses. On reaching the gates to Little Paddock go through the gate to the left of it and follow the path over Lardon Chase. Begin a dramatic climb up the

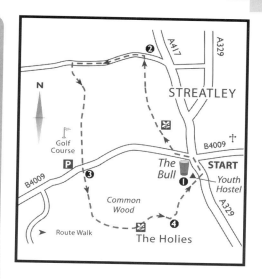

hillside and make for a stile at the top. Keep slightly right on the level ground and drop down the steep slope towards a line of houses. Look for a stile and gate by a white house and exit to the road.

② Turn left, follow the route of the Ridgeway and walk along to Streatley and Goring Golf Club. Turn left just beyond it at some outbuildings and follow a strip of tarmac to a gate and stile in the hedge. Cross a tarmac drive and go slightly left now, following the footpath across the fairways. The path curves gently to the right and up the slope. Pass several waymarks and keep ahead on a path running between hedgerows and grass margins. Look for the warning bell, cross a clear path and head for the trees. Follow a shaded path to the road.

③ Cross over to some steps and a National Trust sign. Follow the path to a kissing gate and galvanised gate, avoid a

Overlooking the Thames Valley

path on the right and go up the steep bank. Keep to the clear path as it crosses The Holies. As you approach a gateway and stile, turn left and follow the waymarked path through the trees.

④ Ignore a path on the left and go down through the trees to an open space. Pause for a few moments to absorb the stunning view and then continue down a flight of shallow steps to reach wooden panel fencing. Descend to a stile and the road just beyond it. Turn left, pass the Youth Hostel and return to the Bull.

PLACES OF INTEREST NEARBY

Basildon Park is a classical 18th-century house by John Carr. The house, which contains some fine plasterwork, various pictures and furniture, a small formal garden and woodland walks, is open to the public between March and October. Telephone: 01189 843040.

Aldworth
The Bell

MAPS: OS EXPLORER 158 & 170
(GR 555796)

WALK 17

DISTANCE: 3¼ MILES

DIRECTIONS TO START: ALDWORTH IS ON THE B4009 NEWBURY TO STREATLEY ROAD. THE BELL IS JUST OFF THE MAIN ROAD, LOCATED IN THE VILLAGE CENTRE AND A LITTLE TO THE NORTH OF THE CHURCH. **PARKING:** THERE IS A CAR PARK AT THE REAR OF THE PUB AND LIMITED ROOM AT THE FRONT. RESTRICTED PARKING ELSEWHERE IN THE VILLAGE.

Whatever the season, most walkers make a beeline for the Bell after a short stroll or a long hike in the surrounding countryside. Soon after starting our walk, stop to have a look at Aldworth's historic church, which is usually open and contains effigies of the 13th- and 14th-century de la Beche family. Known as the Aldworth Giants, there are nine of these stone figures. Elizabeth I is said to have ridden over to Aldworth from Ewelme to inspect the church and its famous giants, some of which are now quite badly damaged.

Almost from the word go, there are spectacular views across miles of windswept downland country and over towards the gentler Thames Valley to the north. The Ridgeway, Britain's oldest road, is seen in the distance, too, and the whole area conveys a sense of space and isolation – perfect for a pub stroll.

The Bell

One of Berkshire's classic inns, the Bell at Aldworth is a gem. Most people in the county have heard of it and many know it intimately. Once you've found the Bell, you never grow tired of it and those who appreciate a truly authentic local, savour its simple format and unchanging character. Step inside and you could be forgiven for thinking you've been transported back in time to a gentler age before piped music, mobile phones and games machines. Among its most striking features are a glass-panelled hatch and a shiny ochre ceiling. The landlady's great grandmother installed the triple beer engine in 1902 and the one-handed grandfather clock has stood in the tap room for 300 years. Sadly, with the pub trade changing virtually beyond recognition, the Bell is something of a rarity these days. No wonder it has been voted CAMRA Pub of the Year on more than one occasion. Hot crusty rolls form the main core of the menu and include ham, Stilton, turkey, corned beef, cheese and onion and Devon crab. Ploughman's lunches and a range of hot and cold puddings are also available, together with several popular ales. Food is served every day except Monday, when the pub is closed (bank holidays excluded). Telephone: 01635 578272

The Walk

① From the Bell cross the road and pass the former village shop and post office. Avoid the turning to the Downs and keep ahead down the lane to Aldworth church.

From the main entrance, with an ancient yew tree on your left, go through a little gate and turn right at the track. Pass a footpath and continue on the concrete byway, keeping to the right of farm outbuildings.

② Cut between fields and as you approach the road look to your right for a glimpse of Aldworth church in the distance. Turn left at the junction and pass a track on the right. There is a good view of Bower Farm here, seen in more detail on the return leg. Continue along the lane to Starveall Barn and look for a footpath on the right. Take it, cross two stiles and keep along the right edge of the field. A curtain of woodland is seen ahead, with the Ridgeway running this side of it.

③ Make for the bottom right-hand corner of the field, turn right and follow the track. When it bends right, swing left to join a byway and keep a fence on the left.

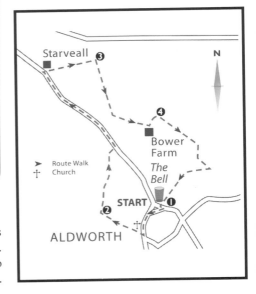

St Mary's church, Aldworth

As you approach Bower Farm, swing left, avoiding a gate and stile leading into the farm, and walk across the field with trees on the right. Pass through a gate and keep right after a few paces at the next junction.

④ Avoid a path leading into a field on the right, pass a sycamore tree and ignore a track on the left. Take the next footpath on the right and cross several fields to reach the rear of the Bell. Follow the shaded path alongside the pub and turn right at the road.

PLACES OF INTEREST NEARBY

Beale Park, near Lower Basildon, is a natural world theme park and among the many attractions are a deer park, steam railway, willow maze and exotic bird collection. Visitors can also picnic on the grass, stroll by the river, go birdwatching or enjoy a spot of fishing. Telephone: 01189 845172.

Hampstead Norreys
The White Hart

MAP: OS EXPLORER 158 (GR 526763)
WALK 18
DISTANCE: 4 MILES

DIRECTIONS TO START: FROM NEWBURY FOLLOW THE B4009 STREATLEY ROAD AND DRIVE THROUGH THE VILLAGE UNTIL YOU COME TO THE WHITE HART ON THE LEFT. **PARKING:** THERE IS A SPACIOUS CAR PARK AT THE SIDE OF THE INN, AS WELL AS A FEW SPACES ELSEWHERE. ALTERNATIVELY, USE THE CAR PARK BY THE RECREATION GROUND.

Almost all the classic features of the countryside are to be found on this delightful walk, which offers a variety of scenery and plenty of good views. As you climb above Hampstead Norreys at the start of the stroll, look across to Folly Hill. During the Second World War this was the site of an airfield, with Wellington bombers based here. Cross farmland and head south, with views over woodland and downland in the distance. On the return leg the walk crosses the pretty little River Pang, which rises near Hampstead Norreys and is famous in the area as a winterbourne tributary of the Thames. Cut through extensive woodland to reach the parish church and, beyond it, the old village well, presented to the people of Hampstead Norreys by a resident of nearby Hawkridge in 1903. The well, no longer in regular use, stands beneath a tiled roof enclosed by wooden palings. The iron machinery for raising water is still intact. Another relic of the past is the Didcot to Southampton railway, which ran through Hampstead Norreys until its eventual closure in 1964.

The White Hart

Dating back to the 18th century, the White Hart was once a Whitbread house and one of several inns in Hampstead Norreys. Today, it is the sole surviving pub in the village. As you enter the panelled bar, the first thing that strikes you is the sense of space. A quaint inglenook fireplace and various exposed beams also add to the charm of the place. Food is available every day and the menu covers everything from snacks to steaks. Main courses include lasagne, omelette, curry and fresh fish such as sea bass and haddock. There is a range of salads and a selection of baguettes. The White Hart offers a children's menu, a choice of daily specials, vegetarian meals and various puddings. Cask ales and lagers can be enjoyed in the bar or outside in the large garden, which adjoins the River Pang. Barbecues are held in summer and inside there is a choice of darts and pool. The pub is open all day on Sunday, when a traditional roast is served. Telephone: 01635 202248.

The Walk

① Turn left out of the pub and then follow the road round to the right. Look for a path on the left, running up to the right of a brick and timber-framed cottage. Follow the signposted path up the steep slope between private gardens and on reaching a field, keep to the left boundary. Make for a bungalow ahead and turn right along the track.

② Turn left at the road and walk along to Firtree Farm. Immediately beyond it join a waymarked path cutting through a tunnel of trees. Pass a gate by a corrugated shelter for animals and keep to the woodland edge. Emerge from the trees and continue ahead across the field, keeping woodland over to the right. On reaching a waymark, turn right and follow the concrete track to the road.

③ Turn right and make for a sharp right bend. To visit the Living Rainforest site keep to the road; to continue the walk go straight on along a tarmac drive. Cross a staggered junction and then head south on a grassy path known as Manstone Lane. Follow the path through a tongue of woodland to reach the road. Turn right and when the road curves gently left, look for a waymark in the right boundary. The path can be overgrown and hidden from view in summer.

④ Cross the stile and go diagonally left to some double white gates in the field

The delightful River Pang

corner. Cross a drive to a stile and head diagonally right over the brow of the hill. Drop down to a stile and telegraph pole in the field corner, cross the road and take the track down to a ford over the River Pang. Take the next right-hand path, follow the field edge into woodland and continue over a junction to merge with a track. Turn right and cross the churchyard to the road. Swing right here, pass the old village well and return to the pub.

PLACES OF INTEREST NEARBY

The Living Rainforest at Hampstead Norreys was established in 1991 on the site of one of Europe's most famous orchid nurseries. In those days it was a privately-run visitor attraction; today, it is an independent registered charity attracting thousands of visitors. Call at the site and you can learn all about the living rainforest environment, as well as the world's endangered plants and wildlife. Telephone: 01635 202444.

Stanford Dingley
The Bull

DIRECTIONS TO START: FROM THE A4 AT THATCHAM FOLLOW THE ROAD TO UPPER BUCKLEBURY. FOLLOW THE SIGNS FOR STANFORD DINGLEY. TURN LEFT JUST BEYOND THE BOOT AND THE BULL IS JUST OVER THE BRIDGE. COMING FROM READING, FOLLOW THE A4 TO THEALE, THEN HEAD NORTH ON THE A340. TURN LEFT TO BRADFIELD. TAKE THE NEXT LEFT AND PASS THE WAR MEMORIAL AND THE QUEEN'S HEAD PUB. TAKE THE NEXT RIGHT TURNING AND TURN LEFT AT THE T-JUNCTION. FOLLOW THE ROAD INTO STANFORD DINGLEY AND THE BULL IS ON THE RIGHT.
PARKING: THERE IS A SPACIOUS CAR PARK AT THE SIDE OF THE BULL.

With its handsome houses and quaint cottages, Stanford Dingley is one of Berkshire's prettiest villages – a suitable starting point for an enjoyable stroll through the charming Pang Valley. In its middle and lower reaches, strengthened by fresh springs, this delightful little river becomes a gravel trout stream meandering through a lush valley. It was on the Pang at Bradfield during the 1860s that children played on crude, home-made rafts, punting down to the village from the Old Rectory and then paddling back once more. Midway round the walk are striking views of Bradfield College, one of Britain's most famous public schools and founded by Thomas Stevens, rector of Bradfield, in 1850. The college's most famous feature is surely its open air Greek Theatre, buried deep in a disused chalk pit and not easily seen from the road.

The Bull

Major changes have taken place at the Bull in recent years. Since taking over in October 2000, the two couples who run this classic country pub have added six well equipped bedrooms and a new dining room which can seat up to 30 people. The Bull may have a new look but it still retains its unique character and individuality. The building dates back to the 15th century and includes a wealth of timbers and even the remains of an original wattle and daub wall. One of the more unusual aspects of this popular inn is the traditional and now quite rare pub game known as ring-the-bull, involving a genuine surviving bull's ring. Food is served every day and the main menu is varied and imaginative, with dishes including roast Barbary duck breast, Hungarian paprika chicken, medallions of pork, Cajun chicken, rack of lamb and seafood chowder. You can eat in the dining room or one of two bars. The traditional tap room, with its red quarry floor tiles and barrel chairs, is a favourite with long-standing customers. Interestingly, there is a splendid painting on the wall of Bradfield College, one of the features of the walk. Several of the popular ales come from the West Berkshire Brewery, a local micro-brewery. Outside is a large beer garden and there are tables and benches at the front. Children and dogs are allowed. Telephone: 01189 744409.

The Walk

① Turn left out of the car park and walk along the road to cross the River Pang. Go straight on at the junction towards Bradfield Southend and Theale and climb the hill until you reach a house on the left called Little Orchard.

② Take the bridleway just beyond the house and follow it down and round to the right through woodland. Avoid paths on the left and right and continue ahead. Emerging from the trees, you'll see charming views of the Pang Valley on the left. Pass a path on the right and keep ahead through more woodland to reach the hamlet of Rotten Row. Make for the road and turn right.

③ Climb quite steeply to a footpath sign on the left by a galvanised gate and an oak tree. Take the path through a tunnel of trees, pass under a bridge and keep ahead to the next road. Cross over to a stile and take the footpath, ensuring you avoid the adjoining bridleway. Follow the path over

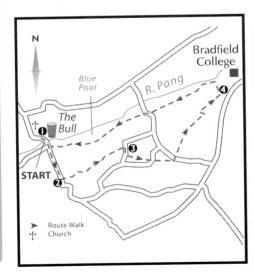

The Pang at Bradfield

paddocks via several stiles and then cut across market gardens to reach the road. Cross over and follow the path across several fields to a kissing gate and drive. Cross it, turning left and then right to follow the path through an avenue of trees beside a golf course. Cross three stiles before turning left.

④ Go over a drive and cross the cricket field to a waymark. Bradfield College is seen to the right. Make for the Pang river bank, turn left and follow the path alongside the water to skirt a large field. Turn right at the road, to the entrance to Bradfield Hall, built in the 1760s for the natural son of George II. Follow the clear path beside it to a track and when it bends

left towards Rotten Row, go straight ahead along a path to a crossroads. Keep ahead through several kissing gates and join a track. Follow it to a gate and keep left in the field to the next gate. Turn right at the road and return to the Bull.

PLACES OF INTEREST NEARBY

The **Blue Pool** at Stanford Dingley, a collection of clear water from natural springs, has long been admired for its colour – a curious, reflective blue. Light is reflected by the particles of mineral glauconite, present in the chalk, which gives the water its blue quality. The pool is well-known in the area and is about 18 feet deep in places.

Beenham
The Six Bells

MAP: OS EXPLORER 159 (GR 586688)

WALK 20

DISTANCE: 3 MILES

DIRECTIONS TO START: FROM NEWBURY OR READING FOLLOW THE A4 AND BETWEEN THEALE AND WOOLHAMPTON. YOU WILL SEE SIGNS POINTING TO BEENHAM, TO THE NORTH OF THE MAIN ROAD. TAKE THE ROAD THROUGH THE VILLAGE AND THE SIX BELLS IS ON THE RIGHT.
PARKING: THE SIX BELLS HAS A CAR PARK. ALTERNATIVELY, IF IT IS NOT BEING USED, PARK IN THE SMALL CAR PARK BY VICTORY HALL IN BEENHAM.

Midway round this very pleasant country walk you reach a magnificent newly-built abbey church at Douai. Work began in 1928 but financial problems delayed work for many decades and it was the summer of 1993 before the church was dedicated. Douai has been at Woolhampton for only 100 years, but its history goes back centuries. In 1615, after the Dissolution, a group of English monks gathered in Paris to form the community of St Edmund. Other English monasteries were formed there and together they restored the English Benedictine Congregation, first established in 1336. The survivors of St Edmund's moved to Douai in 1818 and after they were expelled from their monastery on anti-clerical grounds they crossed the English Channel to Berkshire in 1903. For many years Douai was a well-respected Roman Catholic public school.

The Six Bells

The Six Bells dates back 200 years and has been extended and enlarged on a number of occasions during the last century. Inside, a comfortable bar, log fires and a restaurant add to the appeal of the place, while outside is a popular beer garden. The pub also offers overnight accommodation with rooms overlooking open farmland at the rear. Expect the usual quota of snacks, including sandwiches and baguettes. If you prefer something more substantial, try cottage pie, lasagne or omelette and chips. The menu also features braised beef and vegetables in a red wine *jus*, pan-fried chicken breast wrapped in bacon and stuffed with cheese, grilled lamb cutlets with rosemary and garlic and baked pork chop with braised apples and cider sauce. Fish dishes include poached cod with parsley sauce, grilled swordfish steak and pan-fried tuna loin. Real ales, coffee and tea are also available. No dogs please. Telephone: 01189 713368.

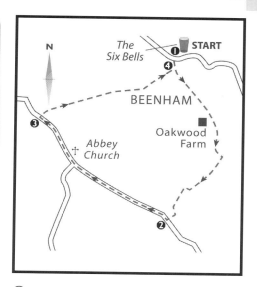

② Keep right and head up the road towards Douai Abbey. Avoid the turning on the left by some thatched cottages and pass the abbey church on the right.

Historic Douai Abbey

The Walk

① From the pub turn left and then right into Clay Lane. Veer left by Jayswood Cottage and follow the byway alongside the entrance to Oakwood Farm. When the track curves left, swing right at the bridleway sign. Cross a stream and turn left. Follow the path round the field, climbing gently by woods to the road. Emerge by the entrance to Malthouse Farm.

Douai Abbey's newly built church

Beyond the church, continue along the road to some cottages and barns.

③ Turn right at a footpath sign and follow the track into the next field. Keep to the edge and when you reach the corner, by the footpath sign, go straight over into the woods. Fields can be seen close by on the left. Follow the path through the trees and eventually reach the outskirts of Beenham.

④ Turn left at the junction, then right by Jayswood Cottage, back into the centre of the village. Retrace your steps to the Six Bells pub or Victory Hall.

PLACES OF INTEREST NEARBY

St Peter's Church at Woolhampton was completely Gothicised in the mid-19th century. The roof and main walls of the old church were retained and the walls encased in flint. The old bell tower was also transformed into a striking shingled spire. Next door to the church and clearly visible from the churchyard is Elstree School, a famous prep school. Prior to becoming a school in 1939, the house was the country seat of the son of an Austrian consul.

East Ilsley
The Crown and Horns

DIRECTIONS TO START: EAST ILSLEY IS NORTH OF NEWBURY AND THE M4. IT IS CLEARLY SIGNPOSTED AND IS A SHORT DISTANCE FROM THE A34. THE INN IS IN THE VILLAGE CENTRE, NEAR THE POND.
PARKING: THERE IS A SMALL CAR PARK AT THE PUB. IF BUSY, PARK IN THE VICINITY OF THE CHURCH.

The month of May is a good time to enjoy this delightful stroll. The trees are in leaf once again, the landscape is plastered with bright yellow fields of oil seed rape and, perhaps best of all, the woods are strewn with hazy carpets of bluebells. Quite simply, everything looks glorious. Exploring some of Berkshire's loneliest tracts of countryside, the walk starts in the centre of East Ilsley, close to the Ridgeway. The name 'Ilsley' comes from the Saxon 'Hilde-laeq', meaning battlefield. It was once known as Market Ilsley, in the days when it was an important centre for sheep sales. The fairs here received a charter from James I in the 17th century and, with the exception of London's Smithfield, Ilsley became the biggest sheep market in England. The fairs died out in the 1930s, though the tradition was revived some years later.

The Crown and Horns

British film actress Susannah York and *The Man from Uncle* actor David McCallum are just two of the stars you might spot in the Crown and Horns in East Ilsley. Look carefully and you'll find photographs of them, along with several other well-known faces, adorning the walls of the pub dining room. But what do they all have in common with the village? In 1991 they appeared in the BBC drama series *Trainer*, which was filmed locally. Set in the world of horse racing, the series was intended as a successor to the glamorous sailing soap *Howards Way*, but it never caught the public's imagination. The Crown and Horns became the 'Dog and Duck'. Not surprisingly, given that it lies in the open country of the Berkshire Downs, a strong racing theme characterises this delightful 18th-century village inn. Various artefacts adorn the beamed rooms, including horse brasses and saddles. Bar food is served every day and there is a traditional Sunday roast. The menu includes imaginative sandwiches in granary bread or wholemeal bap, and various toasties. There is home-made soup, ploughman's lunches and baked potatoes. Other meals include sausage, beans and chips, chicken Kiev and Cornish pasty. There are also grills and vegetarian dishes, a selection of sweets, and a daily specials board. Food is also served in the paved courtyard in summer and there is a separate dining room for which it is advisable to book in advance. Telephone: 01635 281205.

The Walk

① Turn right on leaving the pub, then left by the Swan. Pass under the A34 and turn immediately left at the sign for Stanmore. As the road curves right, join a concrete bridleway running straight ahead. Follow it for about 80 yards, then swing right at the next bridleway sign.

② Keep to the track as it runs out over open downland, avoiding a turning on the right. Pass an isolated barn and eventually the bridleway bends left. Go straight ahead at this point and follow the path across the field to the road at Stanmore. Turn right and walk between various cottages. Pass a turning for East Ilsley and a telephone box and swing right a few paces beyond it to join a byway.

③ Follow it down to a T-junction and turn right. On the left are extensive bluebell woods, best appreciated on a sunny evening when shafts of sunlight illuminate the flowers. At the end of the woods continue ahead on the byway,

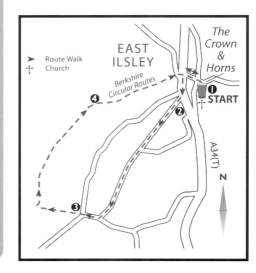

The route follows remote downland tracks

passing a cottage on the left. Keep left at the fork, cross over a track and continue ahead through the woodland. Further on, break cover from the trees and pass Woolvers Barn in a fold of the downs. Pass several left turnings and continue to follow the byway.

④ Keep ahead at the next junction, cut through a tunnel of trees and then between fields to reach the A34 bridge again. Return to the centre of East Ilsley.

PLACES OF INTEREST NEARBY

Farnborough village and its charming church of All Saints lie a few miles to the west of East Ilsley. The church's 15th-century tower watches over the Ridgeway, a mile away, and a beautiful window, designed by John Piper depicts the tree of life. The window is dedicated to the memory of John Betjeman, who worshipped here when he lived in the village after the Second World War.

Bagnor
The Blackbird

| MAP: OS EXPLORER 158 (GR 454694) | WALK 22 | DISTANCE: 3 MILES |

DIRECTIONS TO START: BAGNOR IS ABOUT 2 MILES TO THE NORTH WEST OF NEWBURY TOWN CENTRE. EITHER FOLLOW THE B4000 LAMBOURN ROAD OUT OF NEWBURY AND THEN TURN RIGHT, SIGNPOSTED 'BAGNOR', OR FOLLOW THE DISTINCTIVE BROWN 'WATERMILL THEATRE' SIGNS FROM THE TOWN. **PARKING:** THERE IS A CAR PARK AT THE FRONT OF THE BLACKBIRD. ALTERNATIVELY, THERE ARE SPACES ELSEWHERE IN THE VILLAGE.

This delightfully varied walk is rich in history – both natural and man-made. Not far from the start lie the ruins of Donnington Castle. At the time of the Civil War, this vital stronghold belonged to John Packer, whose refusal of a loan to the King and opposition in Parliament led to the sequestration of his property by Charles I. Colonel John Boys was sent to take command in 1643, withstanding numerous assaults until instructed to surrender in 1646.

Donnington Castle's outline can still be seen but the most impressive feature is its magnificent gatehouse. Further on, you get the chance to stroll across Snelsmore Common, the only country park in West Berkshire. The Newbury bypass protesters have long gone from here but in their place are four-legged residents. Between May and September you are likely to see Dexter cattle, one of the older breeds, introduced to the common to help control tree and scrub invasion.

The Blackbird

There has been a pub here for about 300 years. The present building dates from the 1920s, taking its name from a thatched inn which stood on this site until it burned down early in the 20th century. Over the years the Blackbird has become a regular haunt of actors – many of whom gather here after performing at the nearby Watermill Theatre. I have seen the late Sir Michael Hordern, patron of the theatre, enjoying a drink at the bar, and the actress Josephine Tewson, who gave a memorable performance as Elizabeth the long-suffering neighbour in the highly successful BBC comedy series *Keeping up Appearances*, relaxing with friends and colleagues. Food is available every day except Sunday evening and everything is home-cooked. Among the dishes expect fillet of cod, chilli con carne, lasagne and pasta. Rolls and ploughman's lunches are available at lunchtime and there are various puddings and a traditional Sunday roast. Other than Sunday lunchtime, when the pub can get very busy, booking is not essential. At the side is an attractive beer garden with a play area for children. Telephone: 01635 40638.

The Walk

① Turn left out of the pub and follow the track at the end of the car park. Go through the kissing gate and take the tarmac path up over the A34 to a golf course. Keep left at the fork on the far side of the footbridge, heading towards woodland and an intersection. Cross the

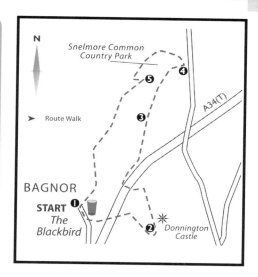

drive and follow a waymarked path on the right, picking your way through the trees. Keep the greens and fairways on the right. Emerge from the woodland at a gate and climb the slope to Donnington Castle.

② Make for a gate behind it, leading to a track, and turn left. Pass between the timber barns of Castle Farm and bear left, following the tarmac bridleway. Re-cross the A34 and swing right, staying on the drive as it dwindles to a track. Keep right at the fork and cut between fences. On

PLACES OF INTEREST NEARBY

The Watermill Theatre at Bagnor is mid-19th century, though there has been a mill here since the time of the Domesday Book. During the 1840s it produced high quality writing paper before becoming a cornmill. In the mid-1960s it was converted into the fine theatre you see today. Over the years the Watermill has earned much respect from the arts world, with various major productions being staged here. Telephone: 01635 46044.

Donnington Castle

the waymarked junction, pass beneath power lines and continue between bracken and gorse bushes. Keep right at the next fork and follow the waymark pointing towards the car park. Merge with another path at the next waymark and as you approach the road, look for a galvanised gate on the left. Go through it to the car park at Snelsmore Common Country Park.

④ Walk away from the road towards a vehicle barrier and a sign for the country park. Veer right at the fork and pass between sunny glades and picnic tables and benches. Follow the track to a kissing gate. Just beyond them the track curves gradually to the left and then runs clear and straight to a left curve. Pass a path on the right here and keep ahead for a few paces to a bridleway.

⑤ Turn sharp right, then veer left at the next fork, avoiding a path on the extreme left. Pass to the right of a seat and descend the steep bank. Cut between trees to a gate and go straight on when the track bends right. Look for a kissing gate on the right and head down the field slope to Bagnor. Make for a gate, turn left at the road and return to the pub.

the left are extensive fairways. Follow the track towards a house standing against a curtain of woodland and keep to the left of it.

③ Pass through a gate and out across Snelsmore Common. Go straight ahead at

Chaddleworth
The Ibex

| MAP: OS EXPLORER 158 (GR 416773) | WALK 23 | DISTANCE: 4½ MILES |

DIRECTIONS TO START: FROM THE B4494 WANTAGE TO NEWBURY ROAD, FOLLOW THE SIGNS
FOR CHADDLEWORTH, WHICH LIES TO THE WEST OF THE ROAD. THE INN IS IN THE VILLAGE CENTRE,
ABOUT HALF A MILE TO THE SOUTH-EAST OF THE CHURCH. IF USING THE A338 FROM THE M4,
GO THROUGH GREAT SHEFFORD, TAKE THE FIRST TURNING RIGHT AFTER ABOUT 1 MILE,
THEN SECOND LEFT TO CHADDLEWORTH. THE INN IS ON THE RIGHT.
PARKING: THERE IS A SPACIOUS CAR PARK AT THE SIDE OF THE IBEX.

This very attractive downland walk links two well-known Berkshire villages – Chaddleworth and Leckhampstead. In places there are impressive views, towards the ridge of hills on the Berkshire/Hampshire border. On reaching Leckhampstead, pause to have a look at the Victorian brick and flint church which was erected by voluntary contribution. Inside, there is a Jacobean pulpit and a 13th-century font which was originally in a Saxon church on this site, demolished in 1860. At the other end of the village the war memorial recalls the men of Leckhampstead who went off to fight and never returned. But this is no ordinary war memorial; it is also a clock with hands made of bayonets, the minutes distinguished by machine-gun ammunition and the Roman numerals made of rifle ammunition. Note the shell cases supported on staddlestones and the chain connecting the stones, which comes from a battleship involved in the Battle of Jutland in 1916.

The Ibex

The Ibex was originally two cottages that formed part of a 17th-century farm. A Grade II listed building, it was later used as a bakery and then as an off-licence before eventually becoming a pub. In more recent years, the Ibex was run by the ex-jockey Colin Brown, who partnered the legendary Desert Orchid for many years. Colin was a familiar face behind the bar, and always took an active role in the day-to-day running of the pub. Inside, the lounge bar is cosy and inviting with a low ceiling, a log fire, bench seats and horse brasses. Adjacent is a small dining room for which it is advisable to book. The restaurant is closed on Sunday evening. Bar meals are served daily (except Sunday evenings) and include ploughman's, steak and kidney pie, sausage, egg and chips, home-made pies, sandwiches and a wide variety of fresh fish. At the rear of the inn is a conservatory and a popular beer garden. Telephone: 01488 638311.

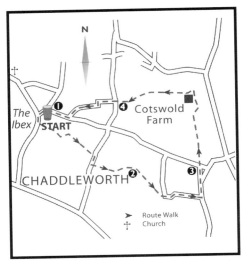

The Walk

① From the Ibex turn left and walk through Chaddleworth, along to a road on the left called Nodmore. Follow the track to the next road and turn right. Take the first footpath on the left and follow it across the field to the next boundary. Cross it into the next field and keep ahead with the hedge on your left.

② At the next junction, by the hedge corner, keep right and follow the grassy path across several fields to a track on a bend. Bear left towards Manor Farm and keep to the right of it. Turn left at the next junction and walk along Shop Lane, through Leckhampstead. Pass the Stag pub and keep left at the war memorial.

③ Pass the speed limit sign and veer to the right of some houses, following a byway which can be muddy. On reaching a track, keep left and head down the slope to a farm. An old wartime Nissen hut can be seen here. Turn left in front of the farmhouse and follow the footpath alongside a paddock. Cross a stile and continue along the field edge beside a barn to a second stile. Turn left and follow

PLACES OF INTEREST NEARBY

Chaddleworth church – if you've time, extend the walk to visit the church, which has a memorial to the Nelson family, a member of whom 'fought two dragoons in the Civil War and was never well afterwards' – according to the church register. Some way further west the path reaches the buildings of Whatcombe, a sizeable stud farm. Look out for the striking bronze statue of Snurge, who won the St Ledger in 1990.

The war memorial clock at Leckhampstead

the field boundary to the third stile. Cross over it and keep right to a fourth stile. Skirt the field, keeping trees on your immediate right. Sloes grow in the hedgerow here. Make for the field corner and continue ahead on a green lane to the road.

④ Walk ahead, following the drive to Oak Ash as the road bends left. As the drive curves left, go straight on to a stile by some beech trees. Cross the field to a gate and follow the drive to the road. Turn right here and head for the next T-junction. The Ibex is on the left.

Boxford
The Bell

MAP: OS EXPLORER 158
(GR 424714)

WALK 24

DISTANCE: 3 MILES

DIRECTIONS TO START: BOXFORD LIES TO THE NORTH OF THE A4 BETWEEN NEWBURY AND HUNGERFORD. APPROACHING FROM NEWBURY, FOLLOW THE A4 WEST AND AT SPEEN, WHERE THERE IS ACCESS TO THE A34 BYPASS, JOIN THE B4000. GO THROUGH STOCKCROSS AND TURN RIGHT AT THE SIGN FOR BOXFORD. THE BELL IS OPPOSITE YOU AT THE NEXT T-JUNCTION. **PARKING:** THERE IS ROOM FOR CUSTOMERS TO PARK AT THE PUB BUT PLEASE TELL THE LANDLORD IF YOU INTEND LEAVING YOUR CAR HERE WHILST DOING THE WALK. THERE ARE LIMITED SPACES ELSEWHERE IN THE VILLAGE.

This very pretty stroll across the floor of the Lambourn Valley and then up on to its north-facing slopes is a delight in any season. Before starting the walk, have a look at Boxford, considered to be one of Berkshire's loveliest villages and boasting a fine assortment of quaint cottages and period houses. At the centre of this community lies Boxford Mill, mentioned in the Domesday Book and now a private house. The thatched cottage opposite, its garden running down to the River Lambourn's edge, was once a bakehouse. The walk crosses the route of the former Lambourn Valley Railway, which closed in 1959. For many years the line was a vital link for the people of the valley, as well as for scattered equestrian and agricultural communities further afield. Though long defunct, the old line is still recognisable in places.

The Bell

The Bell is a popular, well-established mock Tudor country inn and hotel with a strong emphasis on food, all of which is home-made and available every day both at lunchtime and in the evening. There are light meals and snacks, including salads, burgers and ploughman's lunches, and similar fare. To complement the food is a choice of four real ales and an impressive wine list, with champagne by the glass. The Bell received the AA's Wine Pub of the Year award for 2001. The bistro-style blackboard menu offers the likes of lemon chicken risotto, steak fillet à la Bell, lobster, salmon, baked haddock and Thai curry. On Sunday there is a traditional roast. The Bell has eleven bedrooms and an attractive beer garden. Well-behaved children and dogs are welcome. Telephone: 01488 608721.

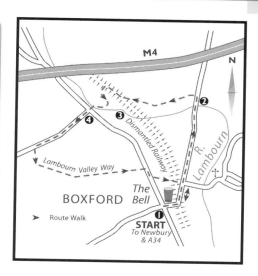

The Walk

① From the Bell turn immediately left at the sign for Chaddleworth, passing the disused Lambourn Valley railway. Follow the road as it bends left and when it swings right, go straight on along the lane leading to Westbrook, passing a varied range of picturesque houses and cottages.

② Cross the pretty River Lambourn and continue to the buildings of Westbrook Farm. Turn left and follow the path along the field edge. Lack of use can make this stretch of the walk a bit overgrown in places, especially in the summer. Make for a stile in the corner and then head

diagonally across the next field, looking for a house among the trees.

③ Draw level with the building and go straight across the next field, passing under power lines. Follow the hedgerow and look for a stile on the left, leading to the old railway line. Cross it to a squeeze stile and head towards the buildings of Eaton Farm. At some barns and a galvanised gate, go straight ahead along the drive. Pass some wrought iron gates at the entrance to the farmhouse and cross the river once again. Make for the

PLACES OF INTEREST NEARBY

Hamstead Park, to the south of the A4 between Newbury and Kintbury, is stately English parkland at its best. It was Sir William Craven who built a magnificent mansion here in 1660, said to have been modelled on Heidelberg Castle. The house was destroyed by fire and all that is left are several sets of crumbling gate piers and some overgrown castle mounds. Various rights of way cross the park.

The river Lambourn – one of Berkshire's prettiest rivers

T-junction and take the lane opposite, following it uphill.

④ Stay on the road as it crosses high ground, cutting between trees and hedgerows. Turn left on reaching a footpath sign, join a track and soon the walk coincides with the route of the Lambourn Valley Way. When the track bends right, go straight on alongside a line of trees. Continue ahead at some waymarks, passing a strip of woodland. Keep to the right of a hedgerow and follow the Lambourn Valley Way down to a gap in the hedge. Turn right at the road for about 100 yards, then swing left into the field. Aim slightly right and make for a stile. Recross the old railway line, descend some steps to the road, turn right and return to the Bell.

Wickham
The Five Bells

MAP: OS EXPLORER 158
(GR 394718)

WALK 25

DISTANCE: 2¾ MILES

DIRECTIONS TO START: FROM NEWBURY FOLLOW THE A4 THROUGH SPEEN TO THE A34 BYPASS. DON'T JOIN IT, INSTEAD TAKE THE B4000 LAMBOURN ROAD AND PASS THROUGH STOCKCROSS TO REACH WICKHAM. THE PUB IS ON THE RIGHT.
PARKING: THERE IS A CAR PARK AT THE FRONT AND THE SIDE OF THE FIVE BELLS.

No walk is complete without a visit to a country church and I have done my best to include as many as I can in this guide. Sadly, in this more brutal world, some churches have to be locked, though you can usually obtain a key locally. One church that keeps its doors open is St Swithun's at Wickham. You reach it almost at the end of the walk but do try to make a point of looking inside. You'll be surprised by what you see. Open the main door and there they are – eight papier-maché elephants peering down at you from the carved oak roof. Apparently, the local vicar, the Reverend William Nicholson, visited the Paris Exhibition of 1862 and found himself captivated by three model elephants which became known as Fortitude, Docility and Strength. Such was his fascination for them that he brought them back to Berkshire, intending to install them in his drawing room. The Reverend Nicholson's wife considered this a rather bizzare idea, so he chose the church instead to display them, commissioning another five to add to the exisiting three.

The Five Bells

Looking at the outside of this quaint thatched inn it comes as no surprise to learn that it is 400 years old. Inside you can picture how it must have looked in bygone centuries when farm labourers and sheep drovers were among the regulars. Today, it attracts custom from Newbury and other nearby towns, as well as those involved in the racing world at Lambourn to the west. The bar is cosy and attractive, with lots of beams and brickwork. If you want a snack, then the Five Bells has a choice of baguettes – BLT, jumbo sausage, ham and mustard, prawns with seafood dressing, tuna mayo, brie and bacon and Stilton and mushroom are among the appetising fillings. There are more substantial dishes, including Mississippi-style chicken breast, lasagne and a traditional Sunday roast. A range of daily specials is one of the pub's more popular features. There is no food on Sunday evening. Children and dogs are welcome. Large parties please book. Telephone: 01488 657894.

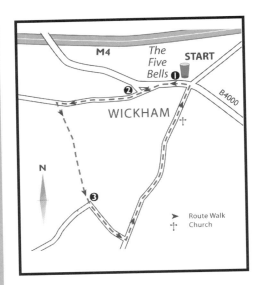

The Walk

① From the Five Bells turn right and walk along the B4000 to a footpath sign on the left. Follow the narrow lane parallel to the main road and when it bends right, go straight on, keeping to the right of a gate and avoiding a path on the left.

② The route now coincides with Windingwood Lane, pleasantly shaded by trees. On the left are glimpses of the hills and dramatic downland which straddle the Berkshire/Hampshire border. At a waymarked bridleway on the left, follow the path as it strides out across the fields, heading south into remote border country. Further on, the bridleway becomes enclosed by trees, bracken, nettles and undergrowth before reaching the road on a bend.

③ Go straight on, passing a pair of semi-detached houses and Orpenham Farm on the right. Look closely and you'll see the barn is supported on staddlestones. Glimpses of the downs continue to enhance the scene. Look for a striking

PLACES OF INTEREST NEARBY

Welford Park, just up the road from Wickham, is just the place to visit if you like flowers. The park is open every February, when its extensive drifts of snowdrops create a dazzling spectacle. The little church of St Gregory has an octagonal spire and a rare round tower. Telephone: 01488 608691.

St Swithun's church, Wickham

house on the corner at the next junction. Turn left at this point and follow the quiet lane back to Wickham, passing the church on the right just as you reach the village. On reaching the B4000, turn left for the Five Bells.

Great Shefford
The Swan

MAP: OS EXPLORER 158 (GR 384752)

WALK 26

DISTANCE: 2³/₄ MILES

DIRECTIONS TO START: GREAT SHEFFORD LIES ON THE A338 BETWEEN HUNGERFORD AND WANTAGE. THE SWAN IS IN THE VILLAGE CENTRE. **PARKING:** THERE IS A CAR PARK AT THE INN BUT PLEASE CHECK WITH THE LANDLORD BEFORE STARTING THE WALK. IT IS ALSO POSSIBLE TO PARK ELSEWHERE IN THE VILLAGE, THOUGH PREFERABLY NOT ON THE A338.

Great Shefford's charming riverside setting makes it a popular destination for hardy ramblers and those who just want to enjoy a leisurely stroll. The walk begins by following a section of the 22-mile Lambourn Valley Way, which was opened by the distinguished actor Sir Michael Hordern in 1992 and is one of my favourite long-distance trails in the region. This popular route enjoys a constantly changing backdrop of spectacular downland scenery, beginning in the centre of Newbury and passing through some of the prettiest villages in the county before terminating on the Berkshire/Oxfordshire border at Uffington. Long stretches of the trail are close to the River Lambourn as typified by this enchanting, easy walk. At Maidencourt Farm, you start heading back towards Great Shefford, passing the village church with its rare round tower *en route*. Charles I apparently spent a night at the adjacent manor.

The Swan

This 200-year-old coaching inn is a very popular village local, though it also appeals to a much wider clientele. Inside are two bars – lounge and public – a dining area and a delightful riverside terrace with views along the River Lambourn, where pretty sycamore and willow trees reach out across the water. The terrace is very popular in summer, when barbecues are a welcome feature here. As well as a good range of real ales and lagers, the Swan's menu is extensive and includes various specials and light meals. Among many other dishes expect tuna penne, spicy chicken tikka, wholetail scampi and lamb steak. For something lighter, try one of the home-baked filled baguettes, a baked potato or a ploughman's lunch. On Sunday there is a traditional roast. Telephone: 01488 648271.

PLACES OF INTEREST NEARBY

Lambourn – this nearby town is worth close inspection. Alfred the Great is reputed to have lived here. Until about a hundred years ago there was a market in Lambourn and at that time it was known as Chipping Lambourn. The splendid church has Norman arches and a chapel containing the parish stocks which used to stand in the adjacent Market Square.

tree-enclosed river on the left. Cross a track and continue along the field edge. Make for a stile, cross into the next field and look for a kissing gate in the left boundary. Turn immediately right to the next gate and keep beside the river. Cut between reeds and go through several more gates to reach the drive to Maidencourt Farm.

③ Turn left and look for a stile on the left. Cross the field, heading towards a stile in the line of trees. Join an enclosed path

The Walk

① On leaving the pub, turn right and follow the Wantage road. Cross the River Lambourn at the footbridge, then swing immediately left to join a path enclosed by fences. At the junction with River Way, cross the road bridge and swing left.

② When the road curves right, go straight ahead, following the Lambourn Valley Way between fences and hedgerows. Skirt a large field, keeping the shallow,

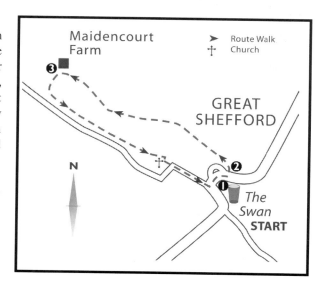

The tranquil River Lambourn

running alongside a house and garden. Cross the next stile and head towards Great Shefford church. Make for a stile to the left of it and pass alongside the church to reach a track. Turn right, then swing left by an avenue of limes leading to an arch at the entrance to the church. Go straight on at the road, back to the Swan.

Eastbury
The Plough

MAP: OS EXPLORER 158
(GR 346773)

WALK 27

DISTANCE: $3\frac{1}{2}$ MILES

DIRECTIONS TO START: EASTBURY IS SITUATED A COUPLE OF MILES TO THE SOUTH-EAST OF LAMBOURN. FROM HUNGERFORD AND THE M4 (JUNCTION 14) TAKE THE A338 NORTH TO GREAT SHEFFORD, THEN FOLLOW THE SIGNS FOR EASTBURY. FROM NEWBURY TAKE THE A4 WEST TO SPEEN AND TURN RIGHT ONTO THE B4000. AT THE JUNCTION WITH THE A338 TURN RIGHT FOR GREAT SHEFFORD AND EASTBURY. **PARKING:** THERE IS A CAR PARK AT THE REAR OF THE PLOUGH AND LIMITED SPACE ELSEWHERE IN EASTBURY.

The River Lambourn, which rises on the downs near here, is especially pretty at Eastbury, with its quaint footbridges and swirling swift shallows. As well as the river, the church is worth a closer look. Its splendid window celebrates the life of the Edwardian poet Edward Thomas and his wife, Helen. The window was engraved by Laurence Whistler and, if you look carefully, you can see various features of the Berkshire countryside through it. Helen was widowed during the First World War when her husband was killed in action in France. She lived for 50 years after his death, the last twelve spent here in Eastbury. Towards the end of the walk, look out for the historic Pigeon House on the outskirts of the village. This locally famous octagonal building dates from the 17th century and was camouflaged during the Second World War.

The Plough

Situated at the heart of the village, the Plough is about 250 years old. The pub, a favourite haunt of local walkers and cyclists, is especially popular with hikers on the nearby Lambourn Valley Way. Many return to the pub time after time. Various members of the racing fraternity have been known to frequent the pub over the years too. These days the emphasis is very much on food with a good choice of bar meals and a popular à la carte restaurant which was extended two years ago. In the bar you can enjoy the likes of steak and Guinness pie, chilli con carne, lasagne and fresh fish of the day – delivered twice a week from Cornwall. On Sunday the menu is restricted to a traditional roast. The lunchtime and early evening menu consists of baguettes, burgers and jacket potatoes. Children and dogs are welcome. Bookings are preferred at weekends. Telephone: 01488 71312.

The Walk

① On leaving the pub turn right for several paces, then turn left over the River Lambourn. Go up the track between brick and flint walls and hedgerow and, as it curves right, turn sharp left to join a footpath at a waymark. Make for a field and keep ahead along its boundary to a kissing gate leading into Eastbury churchyard. Cross it to a wrought iron gate and walk ahead alongside the recreation ground to a waymark and path on the left. Follow it between houses and gardens to the road.

② Turn right and walk through the village, keeping the Lambourn beside you. Head towards the T-junction and turn right at a sign 'unsuitable for heavy goods vehicles'. Follow the road, pass Hayfield Court and leave the village of Eastbury behind you. Avoid a footpath on the right and continue to a copper beech hedge just before the entrance to Haycroft Lodge. Pass a path on the left and go up the slope and round to the right.

③ Look for a stile and gate on the left. At the immediate fork turn right through the wooden gate and follow the path diagonally through the plantation. Cross a stile and go straight down the field slope to another stile. Climb to a curtain of woodland, go through a gate and keep to its left edge. Cross a stile and field, going towards trees, veering left to follow a grassy path along the pasture boundary. Pass through a gate and keep ahead on a track to the road.

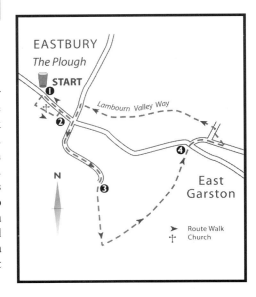

East Garston

④ Cross over and take the turning for East Garston. Turn left by the war memorial, cross a bridge and veer left by some cottages. Follow the road round to the right, then turn left at the Lambourn Valley Way sign. The walk now follows the route of the disused railway track. Make for a flight of steps leading to a stile. Maintain the same direction towards Eastbury, still following the old line, and on reaching some steps running down to the road, turn left. Pass the Pigeon House, cross the road at the junction and retrace your steps to the pub.

PLACES OF INTEREST NEARBY

Ashdown House near Lambourn, managed by the National Trust, dates back to the 17th century and was built as a hunting lodge by the 1st Lord Craven. Tall and ornate, Ashdown is of unusual design, rather reminiscent of a child's dolls' house. The grounds and parts of the house are open to the public from April until October. Telephone: 01488 72584.

Inkpen
The Crown and Garter

MAP: OS EXPLORER 158
(GR 377637)

WALK 28

DISTANCE: $3\frac{1}{4}$ MILES

DIRECTIONS TO START: FOLLOW THE A4 TO KINTBURY, MIDWAY BETWEEN NEWBURY AND HUNGERFORD, AND IN THE VILLAGE CENTRE TAKE THE INKPEN ROAD OPPOSITE THE TURNING TO THE CHURCH. PASS A RESTAURANT AND CONTINUE AHEAD AT THE CROSSROADS. TAKE THE INKPEN COMMON ROAD AND THE CROWN AND GARTER IS ON THE LEFT.
PARKING: THERE IS A CAR PARK AT THE INN, AND LIMITED ROOM IN THE SURROUNDING LANES.

Apart from glorious views over spectacular downland, there are two notable landmarks on this very enjoyable walk. St Laurence's church at West Woodhay was built in 1883 in the style of Early English Revival. Pause here for a few moments of quiet reflection in the charming memorial garden next door. The garden was inspired by Mr Johnny Henderson, father of the racehorse trainer Nicky, in memory of his wife Sarah, who died in 1972, aged 47, following a riding accident. Further on the walk reaches West Woodhay House, the Henderson family home. The house was built by Inigo Jones for Sir Benjamin Rudyard, a poet and eminent politician. He sat for 24 years in Parliament and his famous sense of justice forced him to take a stand against the king during the Civil War. Following his appeal for peace, Rudyard was expelled from Parliament and retired to West Woodhay, where he died in 1658.

The Crown and Garter

The Crown and Garter is a traditional country inn, close to the Hampshire border. The building is thought to be about 400 years old and, though it is hard to believe now, at one time it was a coaching inn when the lane outside was the main coach road to Salisbury. If you enjoy grisly tales of 17th-century child murder, you'll be interested to learn that the adjoining barn was where the bodies of a local man and his mistress were kept after they had been hanged in 1676. George Broomham and Dorothy Newman were found guilty of the murder of his wife and son, whom they ambushed and attacked with cudgels on the nearby downs. After Broomham and Newman had been declared dead, they were taken down from the gibbet on the hills above the inn, where their bodies could be seen from several counties, and placed in the barn until eventually they were taken away for burial. Inside, the pub has a main bar and dining area with beams, a log fire and plenty of character. The imaginative, eclectic menu offers the likes of beer-battered cod, mushroom lasagne and leek and potato cake. There is also a traditional Sunday roast and a children's menu. Booking is recommended, particularly at the weekend. The Crown and Garter is closed Monday and Tuesday lunchtimes, except during school holidays. Telephone: 01488 668325.

The Walk

① From the Crown and Garter turn left and follow the road. Keep left at the fork and follow the road towards Combe and

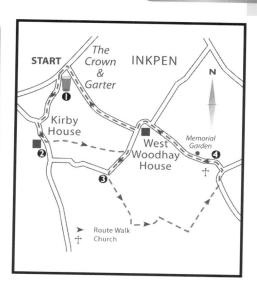

Faccombe. Pass Stockbridge Cottage on the right and on the left the entrance to a Georgian house with a slate roof. Avoid footpaths on the left and right and follow the road down into a wooded dip. Turn left at the junction and pass Kirby House on the right. Begin climbing the hill and turn left at a footpath sign, just beyond a thatched cottage.

② Climb the bank to a stile and branch left in the field, keeping alongside the boundary. Make for a waymark at the end of the trees and hedgerow and continue ahead out across the field. At the road, on the far side, turn right and pass some paddocks on the left. Look for the village sign for West Woodhay and when the road bends right by Park House, keep ahead at the footpath sign.

③ Follow the grassy track as it curves left, cutting between fields. The ridge of Combe Hill and Walbury Hill lies to the south. Head for a curtain of woodland and

The memorial garden at West Woodhay church

follow the track to the right of it, soon swinging left. Keep the trees on the left and climb the slope to the open ground. At a concrete farm track, turn left and make for the road. Turn left and left again at the next junction, signposted to Inkpen and Combe.

④ Pass St Laurence's church at West Woodhay and continue along the road towards West Woodhay House. Pass a turning for Kintbury on the right and follow the road round the left-hand bend, alongside farm outbuildings. Take the next waymarked track on the right and pass some brick and tile-hung cottages. Keep to the track and return to the pub.

PLACES OF INTEREST NEARBY

Walbury Hill, close to the Crown and Garter, is one of Berkshire's most famous scenic attractions. In May 1944, on the slopes of this hill, members of the 9th Battalion of the Parachute Regiment practised for the first assault into occupied France. The plan was to capture the Merville guns which overlooked the D-Day invasion beaches, and a complete replica of the battery was constructed at Walbury. The views from this high ground are breathtaking.

Kintbury
The Dundas Arms

| MAP: OS EXPLORER 158 (GR 386671) | WALK 29 | DISTANCE: $3\frac{1}{4}$ MILES |

DIRECTIONS TO START: KINTBURY IS JUST OFF THE A4, MIDWAY BETWEEN NEWBURY AND HUNGERFORD. THERE ARE REGULAR TRAIN SERVICES TO KINTBURY AND THE STATION IS ONLY A COUPLE OF MINUTES' WALK FROM THE DUNDAS ARMS. **PARKING:** THERE IS ROOM TO PARK EITHER SIDE OF THE CANAL. IF BUSY, FIND A SPACE ELSEWHERE IN THE VILLAGE.

Beginning in Kintbury, this very attractive walk follows the Kennet and Avon Canal and then heads south across country to extensive woodland at Titcomb. The stretch of canal between Newbury and Hungerford is one of my favourites. Here it cuts through some of the loveliest countryside in Berkshire – a landscape of lazy meadows, pleasant wooded hill-slopes and fields. The only thing perhaps to mar its beauty also serves as a reminder of the vital role this canal played in the Second World War. The pill-boxes were strategically placed along the canal bank at a time when Britain braced itself for invasion. Cutting a swathe across England from east to west, the waterway was to act as the second line of defence if the Germans had breached the south coast blockade. Have a look at Kintbury church as you finish the walk. Inside is a memorial to Charles Dundas, who officially opened the Kennet and Avon Canal in 1810.

The Dundas Arms

Built for local canal workers, the Dundas Arms occupies a charming waterside position between the canal and the River Kennet. It has been a pub for over 200 years and today it is also a hotel. Step inside and you'll find a choice of main bar, restaurant and family room. Outside is a most attractive terrace which overlooks the water. In summer this can get very busy, but if you can secure a table here, it is well worth it. The passing narrow boats create a colourful, bustling scene. The menu changes with the season. Expect a good choice of starters and steak and kidney pie, fried scampi, hot smoked chicken, Cajun spiced chicken breast with stir fry and grilled rump steak among many other dishes. There are puddings and children's meals, plus a daily specials board. Food is available every day except on Sundays or on Monday evenings. Children are welcome. Telephone: 01488 658263.

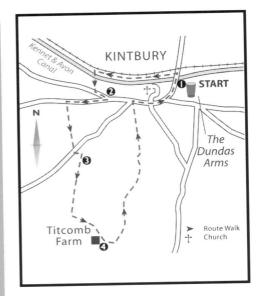

The Walk

① From the Dundas Arms join the Kennet and Avon Canal towpath and head west with the railway line on the right. Pass under a bridge and on the left is the imposing Old Rectory. Cross the canal at the next bridge and make for the road.

② Turn left, then first right and pass the entrance to Inglewood Lodge. Turn left at Kintbury Farm and cross several fields to a minor lane. Over to the right is the outline of Inglewood Health Hydro, set against a backdrop of trees. Turn right and continue for about 50 yards, then turn left over the stile into the field. Swing left and make for some outbuildings and a storage tank beside them. Turn right and follow the grassy track towards woodland.

③ On reaching the trees, you will see a sign – 'Private Woodlands. Footpath to Titcomb Only. Keep Dogs on Leads'. Cross the stile and follow the clear waymarked path ahead. The path runs through the trees that create a pretty picture in any season. After some time you reach a stile at the end of the wood. Continue ahead in the pasture for about 100 yards, aiming for a stile on the left. Cross it, keep ahead along the field edge and make for the stile ahead. Keep a wood hard by you on the right, cross two stiles in the field corner and go forward for a few yards over a stream. Head straight across the middle of the field, keep to the left of some farm outbuildings and join a concrete track.

The River Kennet

④ Keep left and follow the track to a junction. Turn left for Titcomb Manor and when the lane bends left, swing right through a field gateway. Veer left in the field and when you draw level with the manor, swing right across the field, making for the stile in the far boundary. Keep ahead in the next field and then join a path in the corner, skirting woodland. The field should now be on your left. At the end of the path, look for a stile a few yards away and join an enclosed path. On reaching the road, turn right and return to the pub, passing the road to Kintbury church on the left.

PLACES OF INTEREST NEARBY

Hungerford is one of Berkshire's traditional country towns and a great favourite with antique collectors and enthusiasts. The High Street has many antique shops. Hungerford is surrounded by some of the prettiest countryside in the county, and within easy reach of the town is its historic common where you can stroll at will and enjoy this peaceful setting.

Wash Common
The Gun

MAP: OS EXPLORER 158
(GR 458651)

WALK 30

DISTANCE: $3\frac{1}{4}$ MILES

DIRECTIONS TO START: FROM THE CENTRE OF NEWBURY, TAKE THE A343 ANDOVER ROAD TO THE TOP OF THE HILL. THE GUN IS ON THE RIGHT, AT THE JUNCTION WITH ESSEX STREET AND MONKS LANE. **PARKING:** THERE IS A CAR PARK AT THE PUB. IF BUSY, USE THE ADJACENT CAR PARK BY THE SHOPS, OFF ESSEX STREET.

Traffic on the controversial A34 bypass thunders beneath you as you cross the footbridge just outside Wash Common. Elsewhere the countryside has changed little since the first of Newbury's two Civil War battles was fought here on 20th September 1643. This gentle stroll explores the battleground where the Royalist army, commanded by Charles I, and the army of Parliament, led by the Earl of Essex, engaged in bitter conflict. The bloody encounter, in which 6,000 men died, became known as the First Battle of Newbury. As you pass over the slopes that were so brutally contested that day, the imagination can decide at will what the eyes see about them – quiet fields and green hills or smoke, screams, terror and blood. Newbury library holds background information on the battle, which is also described in guidebooks to the area.

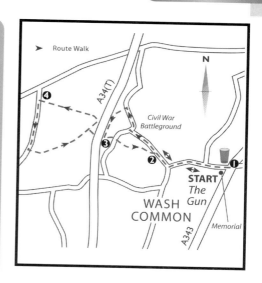

The Gun

Appropriately, the Gun has a connection with the theme of this walk. Apart from the name being a bit of a clue, according to the landlord, there has been a pub on this site since the First Battle of Newbury in 1643. Not surprisingly, the place looks a little different today. Inside you'll find a lounge and public bar, as well as a separate dining area. There is a good menu offering such dishes as mixed grill, steak and kidney pudding, cooked ham, chilli con carne and 10oz rump steak. Various burgers and vegetarian meals also feature and there is a choice of large filled baps. The landlord is a keen real ale enthusiast and a member of CAMRA, so expect six real ales among a selection of other drinks. Large parties are asked to book, children are permitted in the dining area and there is a large beer garden with a play area outside. The Gun is open all day. Telephone: 01635 47292.

The Walk

① From the pub turn right into Essex Street. As you do so, have a look at the 1878 memorial to Lord Falkland, Secretary of State, who died in the early stages of the battle whilst serving as an ordinary trooper. At the age of 33 he was a brilliant young statesman and much admired by both sides. Follow Essex Street until it bends left and then take the lane on the right.

② The familiar sound of traffic begins to fade now as you head into the countryside. Keep right at the next junction and pass a farm on the left. Take the path on the left immediately beyond it and, as the drive curves left, go straight on along a grassy path. Cross a footbridge and stile and follow the path alongside the bypass to the next stile. Continue to the footbridge, where you will find a stile just to the left of it, turn right and cross the A34.

③ On reaching a pair of galvanised gates, keep right at the hedge in front of you and pass a stile on the left after a few paces. Make for a wood on the far side of the field, cut through the trees and head straight across the next pasture to a footbridge and stile. Keep ahead along the field boundary and head for a gap in the top corner. Cross a stile and follow an enclosed path to the road.

④ Turn left and pass Christmas Farm and shop further on. Continue along the lane to the next stile on the left and follow the

The site of the First Battle of Newbury, 1643

path between fences. Cross a footbridge and stile and make for the edge of a field. Turn left and look for a parallel path between trees and hedges. Cross two more stiles and then veer half-right to the A34 footbridge. Cross it and follow the track to the road. Take the path opposite, keep ahead and follow the boundary over two stiles to the lane. Turn right and return to Essex Street.

PLACES OF INTEREST NEARBY

Highclere Castle, home of the Earls of Carnarvon and the largest mansion in Hampshire, was designed by Sir Charles Barry, architect of the Houses of Parliament. 'Capability' Brown was engaged to create the magnificent parkland for which Highclere, located to the south of Newbury, is so famous. Telephone: 01635 253210.